W0254407

EVA SLATER, *NEBULA*, N.D., OIL ON BOARD, DIAMETER (OVAL): 18.5 INCHES, SIGNED VERSO. PHOTO: MARTIN A. FOLB, PHD. FROM *EMERGING FROM THE SHADOWS* (SCHIFFER PUBLISHING)

WHEN WAS THE LAST TIME
YOU READ SOMETHING NEW?
Lose yourself in some of the finest
European graphic novels on europecomics.com
EUROPE COMICS
Co-funded by the
Creative Europe Programme
of the European Union

LOS ANGELES REVIEW OF BOOKS QUARTERLY JOURNAL | SUMMER 2016

EDITOR–IN–CHIEF
TOM LUTZ

EXECUTIVE EDITOR
BORIS DRALYUK

QUARTERLY JOURNAL EDITORS
JONATHAN HAHN, TOM LUTZ

SENIOR EDITORS
DINAH LENNEY, ELIZABETH METZGER, MEDAYA OCHER, MICHAEL URSELL, LAURIE WINER, KATE WOLF

ART DIRECTOR
MEGAN COTTS

ART CONTRIBUTORS
ETHAN COOK, MIKA HORIBUCHI, PATRICK JACKSON, ZACHARY LEENER, PATRICIA LUNA, KYMIA NAWABI, HELEN CLARK OLDFIELD, CHERIE RACITI, ELISE CAVANNA SEEDS, MAUREEN SELWOOD, ADA MAY SHARPLESS, EVA SLATER

PRODUCTION AND COPY DESK CHIEF
CORD BROOKS

MANAGING DIRECTOR
JESSICA KUBINEC

AD SALES
BILL HARPER

BOARD OF DIRECTORS
ALBERT LITEWKA (CHAIR), REZA ASLAN, BILL BENENSON, LEO BRAUDY, BERT DEIXLER, MATT GALSOR, ANNE GERMANACOS, SETH GREENLAND, STEVEN LAVINE, ERIC LAX, TOM LUTZ, SUSAN MORSE, CAROL POLAKOFF, JON WIENER, JAMIE WOLF

COVER ART
L.E. KIM
UM41, 2016
OIL ON PALETTE PAPER
20.5 X 32.25 INCHES (FRAMED)
COURTESY OF THE ARTIST AND KLOWDEN MANN GALLERY

The Los Angeles Review of Books is a 501(c)(3) nonprofit organization. The *LARB Quarterly Journal* is published quarterly by the Los Angeles Review of Books, 6671 Sunset Blvd., Suite 1521, Los Angeles, CA 90028. Submissions for the *Journal* can be emailed to EDITORIAL@LAREVIEWOFBOOKS.ORG.

© Los Angeles Review of Books. All rights reserved. No part of this publication may be reproduced, stored in a retrieval system, or transmitted in any form or by any means, electronic, mechanical, photocopying, recording, or otherwise, without the prior written permission of the Los Angeles Review of Books.

Visit our website at WWW.LAREVIEWOFBOOKS.ORG.

The *LARB Quarterly Journal* is a premium of the LARB Membership Program. Annual subscriptions are available. Go to WWW.LAREVIEWOFBOOKS.ORG/MEMBERSHIP for more information or email MEMBERSHIP@LAREVIEWOFBOOKS.ORG.

Distribution through Publishers Group West. If you are a retailer and would like to order the *LARB Quarterly Journal*, call 800-788-3123 or email orderentry@perseusbooks.com.

To place an ad in the *LARB Quarterly Journal*, email ADSALES@LAREVIEWOFBOOKS.ORG.

CONTENTS | SUMMER 2016

Shorts

Poetry

Features

Fiction

~~niggers~~
~~gooks~~
~~kikes~~
~~spics~~
~~chinks~~
~~porch monkeys~~
~~wet backs~~
~~towel heads~~
redskins

Insult and Brand

C. Richard King

UNPBLOG.COM
NEBRASKAPRESS.UNL.EDU

From the Editor's Laptop

This issue of the Quarterly Journal is the first and the last — the last with executive editor Jonathan Hahn and the first with executive editor Boris Dralyuk. The first without a featured artist, the last without a featured artist (it's a long story).

The lead piece in the journal is also about the first and the last — Anthony McCann, who has spent many years in southeastern Oregon, went back up to the Malheur Wildlife Refuge and the town of Burns to investigate the Ammon Bundy-led occupation and "the complex history of the land they stood on — a history of which the occupiers seemed as definitively ignorant as they were ill-prepared" in general to fulfill whatever they thought their mission was. The Bundy group was the last, or most recent, to lay claim to the land in the Harney Basin; the Tribal Council of the Burns Paiute have reasonable claims to being descendants of the first. The Paiute, McCann reports, offered "the most unambiguous, defiant, and absolute community rejection" of Ammons's usurpation of the Refuge.

A long poem by Nathaniel Mackey, fiction by Azareen Van der Vliet Oloomi and Vanessa Hua, a look at family ties to North and South Korea by Nancy Jooyoun Kim, and report on another contested occupation — in Western Sahara — by Tom Stevenson, along with superb poems and a half dozen new entries into our series of shorts — it is hard to decide what to read first.

Most of you reading this are members of Los Angeles Review of Books (and if you're not, godammit, you should be, if you can afford it). We have a new feature on our membership page for anyone who would like to get more involved with what we are doing. We are still chronically underfunded, the literary world still reeling from its takeover by platforms like Amazon.com and Apple, from the ascendancy of platform over "content" (i.e., the writing we love), and we still need to grow our network of support to stay alive and thrive. Click on the new button — see if there are more ways you'd like to help.

Tom Lutz

TOM KNECHTEL

Astrolabe
New Work

September 17 – October 29, 2016

MARC SELWYN FINE ART

9953 South Santa Monica Blvd., Beverly Hills, CA 90212
www.marcselwynfineart.com

Astrolabe, 2016, etching on Pescia Handmade 300gsm soft white paper, edition of 15, 13 x 24 inches (image); 22 x 30 inches (sheet)
Printed by Anthony Zepeda; Published by CB1 Gallery, Los Angeles

The Reader of His Own Self
Prints and Drawings 1979 – 2016

September 10 – October 30, 2016

1923 S. Santa Fe Ave., Los Angeles, CA 90021
www.cb1gallery.com

Black Gods of the Asphalt

Religion, Hip-Hop, and Street Basketball

ONAJE X. O. WOODBINE

"A deeply personal and poetic travel through the author's own story of racial struggle and the survival tactics of the players he befriends."

—*Publishers Weekly* (*starred review)

Éric Rohmer

A Biography

ANTOINE DE BAECQUE & NOËL HERPE

One of *Publishers Weekly*'s Best Summer Books, 2016

"[A] superb new biography."

—*The New Yorker*

"Biography of the year for cineasts."

—*Booklist* (*starred review)

Hunting Girls

Sexual Violence from **The Hunger Games** *to Campus Rape*

KELLY OLIVER

"[A] compelling exploration of the dark side of the modern fairytale . . . A challenging, disturbing, and enlightening book."

—Barbara Creed, author of *The Monstrous-Feminine: Film, Feminism, Psychoanalysis*

CUP

CUP.COLUMBIA.EDU · CUPBLOG.ORG

"A superb, eloquent memoir that sings with imagery."
—JerriAnn Geller, *Booktrib*

UNPBLOG.COM
NEBRASKAPRESS.UNL.EDU

PATRICK JACKSON, *JOINTS*, 2016. PLASTICINE, POLYURETHANE, EPOXY. 34 x 26.5 x 7.5 INCHES. COURTESY THE ARTIST AND GHEBALY GALLERY, LOS ANGELES. PHOTO: JEFF MCLANE

THANK YOU TO ALL
OUR MEMBERS:
LARB
is impossible
without
you

If you are not yet a member of reader-supported LARB,
please go to http://lareviewofbooks.org/membership

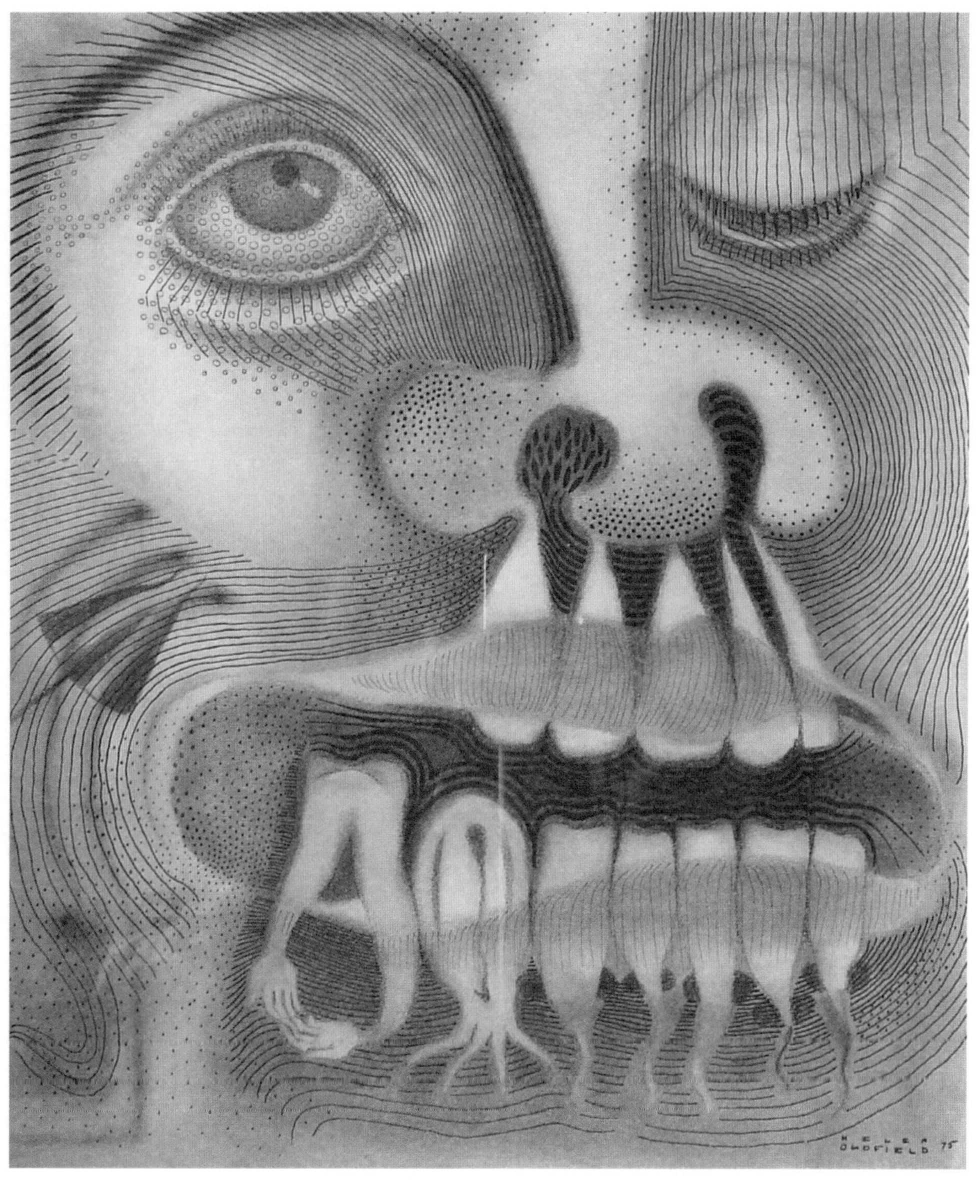

HELEN CLARK OLDFIELD, *TROUBLESOME TOOTH*, 1975. CHARCOAL, PASTEL AND INDIA INK ON PAPER, 15 x 12 INCHES. FROM *EMERGING FROM THE SHADOWS* (SCHIFFER PUBLISHING)

The Mailman

Diana Khoi Nguyen

In an empty room   I sleep
                    the shape of my skull in my hands
      thinking about how to ask God
                    to be nicer.
The sky is bright   as a bowl on a nurse's table
                    then it's as bright
            as the shadow of the bowl.

                                        And my body
      as if detecting
                    a red dress in fog
                    hears the soft shimmer of notes
trembling lighter
                    than the wing
      of a moth   landing on a collar.

            As suddenly as it fills the chamber
      it takes leave.

      What comes unexpectedly isn't

uninvited. A thud   from the chute in the wall –
                    each time the thrum different.
      I lace my sandals   retrieve from the bin of the chute
      a mandolin
            glistening like the flesh of an onion.
                    I wipe my hands on my ashy coat
take her to where

                                        a man who looks like me thanks me
                    for coming again.
      When he lifts her up to play
      the music spills

like a man at his sentencing
                    who having written his own sentence
      doesn't deliver it –

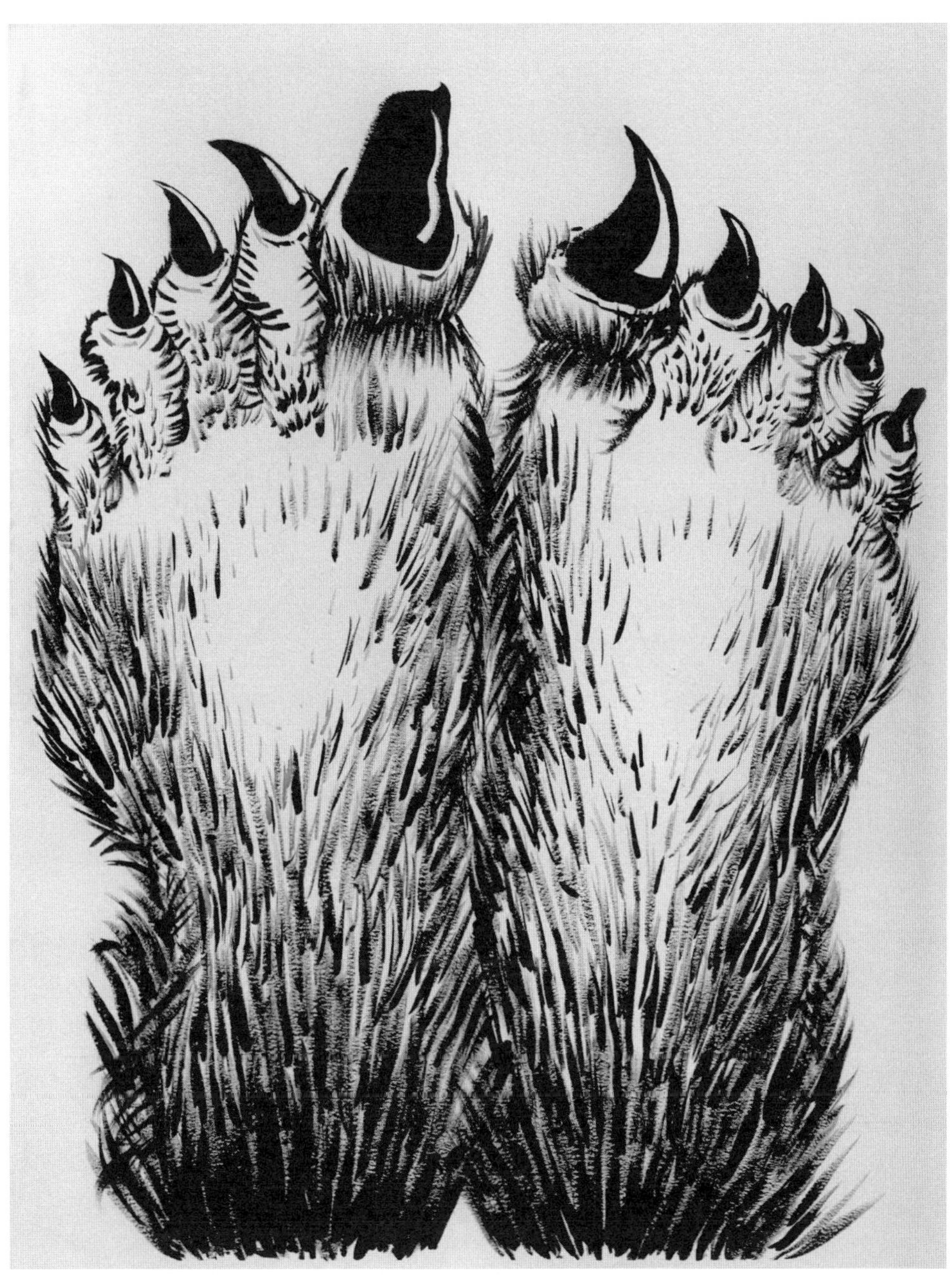

PATRICIA LUNA, *STIGMA*, 2016, COURTESY OF THE ARTIST

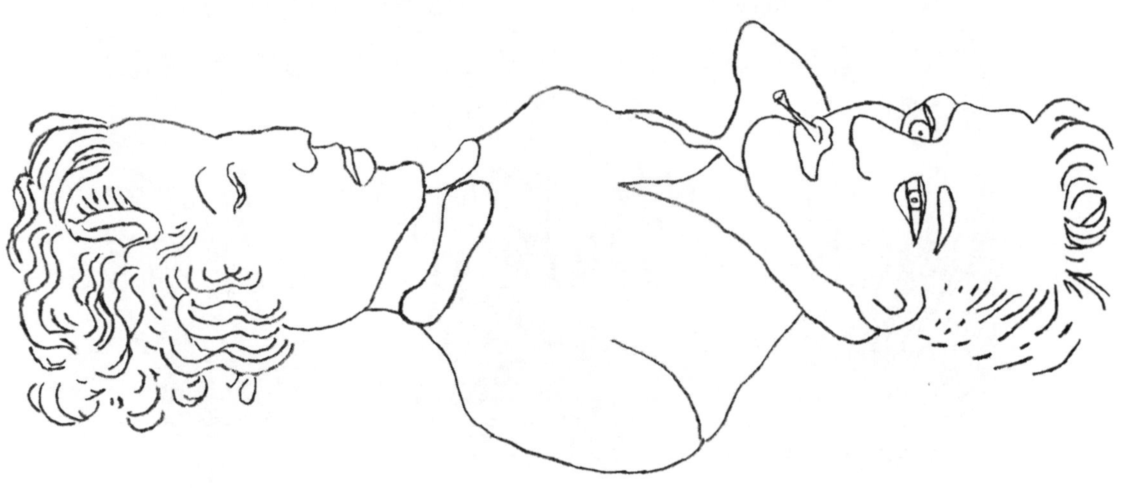

MAUREEN SELWOOD, *CAMUS AND FRANCINE*, 2016, GRAPHITE ON PAPER.

Adrienne Rich: Dream

MICHAEL KLEIN

This is the world you saw: the one now: the one you most resisted: bought and sold,

commodified, hostage-taking. World against ideas; world fractal,

blown up this way every day. There's no breaking out – it breaks *in* now: reloads, recalibrates,

reconsiders the land's mass undertaking. It's dark, and the darkness surrounds

the car I drive – the way I am always driving to Provincetown to see

someone I married one August, in the middle of the street,

where a door opened into a complicated garden; to

see who he is now after two summers of loss and repair or is it

loss infinitum? Sometimes I don't know if I am listening – the way I used to listen

for the weather report of where I was; what I couldn't see.

Years ago, in a summer night high above traffic, between apartments in New York,

you handed me a candle and said *it serves its purpose in a life.*

And here we are, like this together – both living, both dying. Me asking you

in the car's manufactured silence as we snake our way into the last village

of the tour: *Who did this, if we could not do this?*

Malheur

Anthony McCann

Malheur I: Sovereign Feelings

THEY MUST HAVE FELT great out there. Even if they didn't really know much about it, even if they were (and they were) basically lost, it's still an awesome place and it must've been great just to be there. Let's leave aside, for the moment, the question of what a place is, or what it is to be lost, or lost in place; let's stick to the feelings, even if place is a feeling, and even if lost is often how one feels, or finds one's way to feeling. It must have felt grand just to be there in that land, in that 'scape, there where they were — in a territory newly liberated, freshly invented, mapped out by the lines of their activity, of their feelings. After all, they weren't just there, they weren't just in it, they were it — and it, their own new thing, was cradled in all this shimmering enormity.

The Harney Basin of southeastern Oregon, which Ammon Bundy and his brother and their friends had chosen for their armed standoff with federal power, is one of the many basins that make up the Great Basin Desert that stretches over parts of Nevada, Utah, Idaho, and Oregon. It's an affectingly beautiful space, full of all the silence and wind you'd expect. It's the kind of place people call the Middle of Nowhere, where if you look long enough space starts to stare back, as it folds into itself and turns into time. You don't really look at it: you're in it, and being in it is like breathing it in. The wide open sagebrush plains are intersected by swooping lines of hills, volcanic crater rims, and the brooding basalt foreheads of the sage-stubbled buttes. The green sage and golden grasses are occasionally punctuated by the solitary enigma of a craggly juniper tree as the whole landscape tilts down toward the white-blue shimmer of the alkaline lakes of the Malheur National Wildlife Refuge, which the Bundy gang had occupied as the foundational site of their Constitutionalist revolution.

Of course, I don't really know what the Bundy gang felt about the landscape, and they're all locked up now, or — in the case of one — dead, so they're not going to be talking to me about it any time soon. But I suppose if they paused to consider it at all, they are likely to have experienced all that witchy beauty as fate, or Divine Providence's revealed incarnate endorsement of their political theology and mission. One of the last holdouts — the irrepressibly garrulous Sean Anderson — said that he took the ease of the occupation as proof that God was behind it. Maybe Steens Mountain, whose sacred power it is hard not to feel, was a patriarchal ratifier for them, a snowy-headed Founding Father, presiding over the basin from the blue revolutionary distance — white-wigged like the mysterious period-dressed figure who appeared one weekend on the occupied compound of the refuge, as if sprung from the cover of the annotated Constitution all the Bundy boys seemed to carry on their persons at all times.

But however they did or didn't think about it, it still must have felt grand to wake up and see that mountain every morning, to look out over the sage hills, the lakes, and the buttes, and then step out into that space, a territory they were imaginatively remaking with the movements and force of their bodies and minds. And given that the core issue of the occupation was sovereignty, over land and self — wasn't feeling grand what it was all about?

¤

They must have felt great at the very beginning too, on that day, day one — Ammon and Ryan Bundy, LaVoy Finicum, Ryan Payne, and the rest of the boys — pouring out of the town of Burns in their big-assed pickups, flags fluttering behind them, those doctored pamphlets of the Constitution pressed to each of their pounding breasts as they took the turn off Highway 78 onto Oregon Road 205; pouring over the snowy sage land and then up over the volcanic butte at Wright's Point. From there a stunning view of the Harney Basin opened up, as the ribbon of road flowed below them in one of those improbably straight lines you can find so often in the highway borne vistas of the American deserts. It took them directly to the Malheur Wildlife Refuge, and a God-soaked encounter with history and the personal hypostasis they had each conjured of that monstrous abstraction called the United States of America. "Hallelujah!" that State would exclaim — through the mouths of its agents — six weeks later, as it took the last of them into its arms.

¤

The Bundy vanguard's caravan to glory soon ran into some obstacles, some of which would come to visibly hurt their feelings. The famous lack of food supplies, for instance, a product of the inconvenient urgency of divine inspiration. Feelings were publicly injured in the internet mockery that followed their famous plea for "snacks." Still, judging by the girth of supply they left behind, that particular cry for help was overwhelmingly successful in the end. More stubborn — and, to occupation spokesman LaVoy Finicum, fatal — were obstacles presented by the people and history of Harney County. Increasing anger and frustration on the part of many locals, their unity in support of county officials and their rejection of the occupation, eventually gave the FBI the mandate for decisive action it had been awaiting while agents assembled evidence for sweeping federal indictments. On another level, the occupiers were also confronted, and symbolically (or even magically) defeated, by the complex history of the land they stood on — a history of which the occupiers seemed as definitively ignorant as they were ill-prepared.

The history of the territory the Bundy vanguard claimed to have set free was first brought into the media spotlight on day five of the occupation by the voices of the most unambiguous, defiant, and absolute community rejection of their enterprise — that of the Tribal Council of the Burns Paiute. The tribe is an important part of the local community, but the Bundy vanguard didn't seem to even know they existed or had ever existed, judging from their reactions to the tribe's emergence into the conflict at the Tribal Council news conference given on the small reservation at the northern edge of Burns (the county seat), about 30 miles from the refuge. The tribe has historically called themselves the Wadatika — which translates as eaters of wada (seepweed in English) — a plant endemic to the basin, especially to the zone that comprises the refuge, where the Paiute have harvested its seeds for millennia. The occupation of these ancestral lands by groups of armed white men demanding that the territory be turned over to white ranchers to use as they pleased was something the tribe had experienced more than once before.

"For them to say they're going to give it back to the rightful owners, I had to laugh," Tribal Chair Charlotte Roderique said at the conference. "I figured I better write an acceptance letter for when they give it back to us." Tribal Council member Jarvis Kennedy was more direct: "They just need to get the hell out of here." Kennedy also pointedly asked what would happen if he or a bunch of other native people occupied land — land that had actually historically belonged to them. As to the land that comprises the refuge and the rest of Harney County, Kennedy summed up the history thus: "we weren't 'removed'; we were killed and ran off our land."

The story of the Wadatika is full of horrifying violence, inspired resistance, inevitable military defeat, and subsequent awe-inspiring persistence and dedication to the land of the Basin. Their imaginative modes of survival and rejuvenation — what Native American scholar Gerald Vizenor has termed survivance — are characteristic of the history of original peoples all over the continent. "We're the ones who came back," said Roderique, referring to what is called the Paiute Trail of Tears, a brutal forced relocation of the Wadatika and numerous other Northern Paiute bands in the late 1870s. "Nothing could keep us away." The particularities of the story can be chilling, especially in the context of the Bundy takeover. Basically, without exactly "knowing" it, the Bundy boys were performatively recapitulating the entire violent foundational history of Harney County, a place most of them had never heard of until a few months, weeks, or days previously.

For centuries it had all been Paiute land — though, as the tribe takes pains to point out, traditional understandings of the land involve a type of relationship far more intimate than that imagined and codified by private property. "It's more like family than property," said Diane Teeman, the tribe archaeologist. The condition described in "owning land" feels brittle and impoverished indeed if your relationship to the land is closer to the connection you feel to your aunt or to your grandfather, than the one you have with your shoes. White folks had come relatively late to the basin. The first written record of white travel through the territory now occupied by the Wildlife Refuge and the rest of the county is from a fur trading company exploration headed by Peter Skene Ogden, whose expeditions provided initial reconnaissance to Europeans on much of the Great Basin Desert of contemporary Oregon, Nevada, and Utah. Here he is, from his journal, stunned by the size of the population gathered in the traditional camps at the lakes that form the center of the Wildlife Refuge today: "It is incredible the number of Indians in this quarter. We cannot go 10 yds, without finding them. Huts generally of grass of a size to hold 6 or 8 persons. No Indian nation so numerous as these in all North America […] They lead a most wandering life."

While, historically, the description of the lives of Great Basin native peoples as "wandering" has often been used to undermine their claims to their ancestral homes, it is hard to imagine a kind of life with a more intimate claim to land than that practiced by these desert tribes. The Wadatika followed a life of seasonal movements that themselves were part of a reverent, ceremony-filled attention to the land that had sustained their ancestors and their practices for millennia. The archeological record marks out the shape of a persistence of habitation and life practices hard to hold in the mind, as often happens in the deserts of the west, where human temporalities hang out with geologic time. People here, right here, hunted mammoths — and they were still here when the mammoths were gone and the land turned to desert, and they themselves turned to gathering, and to new hunting techniques like those used to catch rabbits in expansive nets in yearly drives, or the ritual magic used to charm herds of antelope so that they entered willingly into earthen pens. They also developed an internal map of the edible roots and seeds of the basin, of its buttes, and slopes, and of the forests in the mountains at the basin's edge.

The circular movement of their years seems to have been powered by pulsations of contraction and diffusion. They came together to winter in temporary villages, near lakes and springs in the basin, as well as, in the height of spring, in camps on sunny hillsides and meadows when the fresh roots of certain key plants, like bitterroot, were tastiest. These root-gathering camps would also be times of joyous assembly, days of dancing, games, foot races — and later, with the coming of the horse, equestrian races as well. Afterward, small family-based bands would disperse into the mountains for summer seed and berry picking, and the tracking of game, all returning later to the lakes to gather other key plants — like their namesake wada seeds in early fall. All this allowed for both a richly varied diet and a richly varied life — if one lived always at the edge of subsistence. At the center of this life was an intimate relation to all the spaces through which they moved; rituals for passing through each type of landscape in the basin and the surrounding mountains are still practiced by members of the Burns Paiute tribe to this day.

The first catastrophic disruption of this traditional life came, predictably, shortly after Skene's expedition, when waves of disease swept through the basin. After the trappers and their diseases came, of course, the settlers and ranchers — the arrival and claims of whom the Bundy gang seemed intent on reenacting in some finally definitive new way, there on the haunted land. Burns Paiute tribal archeologist Diane Teeman brought up the Skene description of the Wadatika population with me, adding, "the fact that there were really so many of us, that so many of us died — this is something that I think continues to be too painful for most people to face. The erasure of that dying is almost complete."

Much of that dying would have happened in the basin by the lakes, when life was hardest and when the people were gathered together in the greatest numbers in their winter villages. Many of those who died were buried there, in that land chosen by Ammon and the boys as their winter camp, to hunker down in with their donated packaged snacks, their Pop-Tarts and Doritos and French Vanilla Creamer, while nodding piously about the Constitution and replenishing their neo-settler bodies with the collective sentiment that bound them in their loose confederacy. Again, they seemed to know nothing of this. When confronted with this history, Ammon Bundy could only say, "that's interesting, I don't know anything about that." After pausing, he added, "but they deserve to be free too."

¤

The entrance of the Burns Paiute into the dispute troubled the leadership of the Bundy militia in a more significant way than any other issue that surged up during the principal period of the occupation. Their response to growing and widespread opposition to their actions in Burns among other sectors of the community, on the other hand, seems to have been an unwavering faith that their vocal supporters in the county were the true majority, as one by one they continued to prod local ranchers to take advantage of the opportunities they were offering. "Now is the time [...] [W]hen will you stand up if not now? If you are not willing to put everything on the table for freedom, are you worthy to have freedom?" exhorted the group's one practicing rancher, the gaunt cowboy Finicum, sounding a little more scripted and fanatical than usual at a public meeting with 30 local ranchers at the hot springs in Crane, a little north of the refuge. "It's a once in a lifetime opportunity; it will never happen again," said the more pragmatic, relaxed, and genially bearded Ammon Bundy, referring to vague nascent plans to allot each rancher their federal grazing area through the county government (the same county government that was actually opposing the whole Bundy operation and calling for their forcible removal and arrest).

The Indians, however, were something else altogether. They refused to speak with the Bundy crew at all, not wanting to grant them any legitimacy, while offering a history that totally undermined the Bundy's own made-up history. That made-up history claimed to show that the lands of the refuge had somehow originally belonged to ranchers who were dispossessed in the early 20th century by Teddy Roosevelt's creation of an "Indian reservation (without Indians)," to quote the Bundy Ranch website. The alleged fake reservation was, in the Bundy story, merely the pretext for a federal land grab in the name of allegedly endangered birds (birds that were actually being hunted to extinction for their feathers by outsider professionals seeking big paydays from the hat industry). As is often the case in conspiracy theories, elements of historical truth stubbornly poked through the faked-up Bundy history, like the obsidian shavings, tools, baskets, and points that constantly emerge from the dirt of the Malheur Refuge. Yes, Indians were involved in this history, but they weren't fake, and now they had shown up. It turned out there had been a real reservation — one the federal government had actually dissolved at the demand of an earlier generation of white ranchers and settlers.

The Malheur Reservation, which originally stretched from the north shore of the Malheur Lake up along the basin's edge and into the northern foothills and mountains, was created to give refuge to all the northern Paiute bands of the Great Basin, who were facing massacres by bands of "volunteers" and starvation, as the fragile ecosystem of the desert was pushed to its limit. There simply wasn't enough to go around as white settlement increased.

All this is vividly documented in *Life Among the Paiutes*, a surprisingly little-known book by one of the most fascinating people of the American 19th century — Sarah Winnemucca. Sarah was the daughter of the important Paiute leader Winnemucca and the granddaughter of an equally influential leader, called Captain Truckee by whites, who had befriended and guided John Fremont in his explorations, and come to identify the true source of white power in the "talking rags" they communicated with. Before dying in old age of a tarantula bite, he had sadly lived to see his hopes for peaceful White-Indian coexistence crumble. Nonetheless, at his request, he was buried with his favorite talking rag, a letter of praise from Fremont. He'd pushed his granddaughter throughout her youth to learn to read and write English — thus, as an adult, she came to be employed on the short-lived Oregon reservation as a translator. Short-lived because local ranchers began encroaching on it and demanding its abolition almost immediately. After a brief happy time, under the atypically competent and sympathetic administration of Agent Samuel Parrish, much beloved by Sarah Winnemucca, her father, and the rest of the Paiute on the reservation, settler pressures led to the installation of a new agent, a local merchant, William Rinehart, who was notoriously hostile to native populations, and evidently as corrupt as he was incompetent. The US army would eventually blame him for much of the desperate calamity that was to ensue.

Within months of Rinehart's arrival, the Indians on the reservation began to starve and, by summer 1878, had fled to Steens Mountain where they were swept up in the grand arc of flight toward Canada known to history as the Bannock War. In the dark days before fleeing starvation on the reservation, Wadatika leader, Egan, for whom much in Harney County is named, gave the following speech. It was translated on the spot by Sarah Winnemucca and later included in her book.

> Did the government tell you to come here and drive us off this reservation? Did the Big Father say, go and kill us all off, so you can have our land? Did he tell you to pull our children's ears off, and put handcuffs on them, and carry a pistol to shoot us with? We want to know how the government came by this land. Is the government mightier than our Spirit-Father, or is he our Spirit-Father? Oh, what have we done that he is to take all from us that he has given us? His white children have come and taken all our mountains, and all our valleys, and all our rivers; and now, because he has given us this little place without our asking him for it, he sends you here to tell us to go away. Do you see that high mountain away off there? There is nothing but rocks there. Is that where the Big Father wants me to go? If you scattered your seed and it should fall there, it would not grow, for it is all rocks there. Oh, what am I saying? I know you will come and say: Here, Indians, go away; I want these rocks to build me a beautiful home with!

Seated listening to Egan as he spoke was a figure I find most intriguing in this history so full of fascinating people living moments of continual crisis: Oytes, shaman and leader of a band of southeast Oregon Paiutes; also a practitioner and proponent of the Dreamer religion. The sect, which had originated in previous decades to the north on the Columbia Plateau, rejected farming and the private individual ownership of land as unethical, insupportable violations of the earth that potentially blocked access to the spirit world, as well as access to the coming new earth, where the dead and living would mingle, and whites would be no more.

Egan was not to live long after giving this speech. Soon he and many of his people would be pulled into the revolt of their neighbors and relatives, the more famously resistant, buffalo-hunting Bannock. The mass movement of the Bannock War, of thousands of men, women, children, and horses — across the deserts into the secret valleys of Steens Mountain, and from there out again between the buttes and over the hills and flats of the basin, up into the Strawberry Mountains where they met their final defeat — was breathtaking in its momentum and scope. The logistical talents of the Bannock and Paiute bands — at this point under the somewhat reluctant command of Egan who had replaced slain Bannock leader Big Horn — befuddled the army pursuing them under the perhaps equally reluctant leadership of General Oliver Howard, former head of the Freedmen's Bureau and the man after whom Howard University was named. When the Bannocks and Paiutes had reached the Umatilla homeland, in the mountains north of the Harney Basin, Umatilla leaders, feigning willingness to join Egan in flight, met with him and killed him for a reward. His head was taken as a souvenir and, after much travel, ended up in Washington, DC. Not until 1993 were the Wadatika able to bring his head home. From his contemporary Burns Paiute reservation gravesite, Egan was to slip secretly into the decidedly more symbolic and spiritual warfare of January 2016.

¤

Ammon Bundy's wishes of "freedom" for the tribe, which accompanied his profession of ignorance of their existence, were quickly undermined by his own brother, Ryan, who was widely quoted as saying that the Paiute had "had the claim to the land, but they lost that claim." He followed up his might-makes-right assertion with a further justification that rang strange coming from an armed reactionary: "the current culture is the most important." The Bundy movement certainly seems more a war on the current, dominant culture than a defense of it. Its popular appeal (and as silly as the occupiers seem to many, they have inspired thousands and thousands of people) relies on its radically conservative, lone-cowboy-in-the-desert style and stance. Their movement coalesces for the first time, in the figures and principles of patriarch Cliven Bundy and his boys, three elements of the radical right: the Mormon Constitutionalist and Sovereign Citizen movements, and the so-called Sagebrush Rebellion.

The Sagebrush Rebellion, sporadically ongoing since the 1970s, has taken many forms in its pushback against any impingement on the priority of ranching life west of the Rockies — a priority the Bundys insist is mandated not only by the Constitution (which is confusing given the absence of cow-herding from that document) but also by the holiness of ranching as a pursuit. According to the Bundys, the first people to receive the word of God were cattlemen. The fact that ranching life often seems, in the gaze of the current culture, a quaint vestige of the Old West doubtless adds to the tragic appeal of Sagebrush rebels like the Bundy gang for the much larger patriot community.

The larger contemporary Sovereign Citizen and Mormon Constitutionalist movements are much richer in conspiracy and magic. The two have many common historical roots stretching back to the Posse Comitatus ("the Power of the County") white supremacist militia of the 1970s and the Mormon fundamentalist Constitutional theories of right-wing scholar Cleon Skousen — a favorite thinker of Glenn Beck, Ben Carson, and Orrin Hatch — whose annotations and often misleadingly selected or altered quotes graced the pocket Constitutions carried by many members of the Bundy gang at Malheur. The many articulations of Sovereign Citizen and Constitutionalist ideology share a rejection of the authority and even the existence of the post–Fourteenth Amendment federal government, and, in many of its versions, including those seemingly practiced by Cliven Bundy and his crew, a vision of true Constitutionally sanctified citizenship only accessible to whites.

These beliefs carry with them a need to rewrite the history of slavery in the United States: Ryan Payne, for instance, is known to have said that he doesn't believe slavery actually happened; Cliven Bundy, along with Skousen, has said he believes slavery may have been a better deal than freedom "for the negro." The "true citizenship" imagined by the

"SovCit" movement — which is often, but not always, exclusively white — is figured as a state of divinely enforced and endorsed being; something called "natural law" is invoked as often as the Constitution, speaking up when that document falls mute. In some sectors of the movement, the state of grace that is Sovereign Citizenship is believed to be accessible in this life through an ornate sequence of legal operations known as "redemption." The correct performance of these operations liberates the SovCit from the admiralty law governing the United States since the Fourteenth Amendment, and places them under the authority of the "true" Constitution. For some, this process also promises adherents access to occult funding streams — namely, the collateral accounts the US government is alleged to have been setting up in the name of each child born in the country since the end of the gold standard, in order to guarantee the dollar.

Clearly, white panic plays a major role in all of this, even when that role is not overt. As the last few years have taught us, for many white folks the very idea that black lives might matter can only be read as an existential threat: a popular chant of pro-Bundy supporters in Harney county was "ranchers' lives matter." That this particular back-to-the-Constitution thing begins with Skousen and others in the 1960s, when the federal government starts intervening to protect the rights of nonwhite persons, is not a coincidence.

Threaded through the Sagebrush-SovCit-Constitutionalist ideological stance forged so successfully in the heat of the 2014 Nevada Bundy Ranch standoff — which brought the Bundys together with many of the participants in the Malheur occupation — are elements of Mormon history and faith that form a mythological understanding of the American past that was also in play in the Malheur pageant. According to the Bundys and many fundamentalist-leaning Mormons, including Bundy intellectual forefather Cleon Skousen and his friend and supporter, former LDS church president (and secretary of the interior under Eisenhower) Ezra Taft Benson, the Constitution itself is a divine document. Cliven Bundy has taken this claim a step further and actually asserted that it was written by Jesus himself. Comments by Ammon Bundy and others reference the famous "White Horse Prophecy," rejected as apocryphal by the leadership of the Church of the Latter-day Saints, but still widely held as credible in the West. The prophecy, allegedly received by Joseph Smith in his dying days, foretells a time when the Constitution will "hang by a thread" and it will be up to the Latter-day Saints to save the United States. Apparently, for the Bundys and their associates, that time had come, and with the urgency of the moment, and the time compressions and recapitulations that characterize the apocalyptic and messianic, figures of the past began to return, voices in the desert, preparing the way for the true reign of the Constitution. A pair of these were sighted by reporters in the first days of the occupation.

¤

On day two of the occupation, one of the first reporters to arrive at the compound came across one lone militant guarding the entrance — a figure straight from the official mythology of the Latter-day Saints (regarded by the church as true American history). The man, identified after his arrest weeks later as Dylan Anderson, at the time gave his name to the reporter as Captain Moroni from Utah, adding, "I didn't come here to shoot, I came here to die." Soon after, a wave of articles on the Bundys, Captain Moroni, and

Mormonism rolled over the internet. Googling Captain Moroni, a key figure from the Book of Mormon, was an education in itself.

First off, it's not Captain Moroni, it's Chief Captain Moroni, as the grandfather explains to the cutely eager, blindingly blond grandson he surprises going through the leather, brass, and glass fetishes of masculinity on the desk in his study in the opening of the official LDS video I found on YouTube. The boy has just accused his grandfather of being a real hero — he's dug up the World War II memorabilia — but Grandpa, of course, must disagree. He was just doing his duty, et cetera — but he'd be glad to tell the tale of a real hero if his grandson would like to learn. As he opens up the weathered Book of Mormon he picks up from his desk, and reads the following passage, his eyes grow more intense: "Yea, verily, verily I say unto you, if all men had been, and were, and ever would be, like unto Moroni, behold, the very powers of hell would have been shaken forever; yea, the devil would never have power over the hearts of the children of men." As he reads, the study scene fades into a clamorously violent, expensively produced battle scene, in a forest of trembling aspens, between sturdy white warriors clad in standard Hollywood ancient warrior garb (picture *Braveheart* or *Gladiator*) and a fleet horde of somewhat darker-skinned fighters, whose Magua-esque hairstyles, clothing, and weaponry mark them, anachronistically — unless you are familiar with the Book of Mormon's North American prehistory — as Native Americans. These, Grandpa explains, are the Lamanites, and they have come to make war on Moroni's Nephites, a peace-loving people with a peace-loving leader who find themselves unwillingly drawn into war.

In the history outlined in the Book of Mormon, both Lamanites and Nephites are Children of Israel who came to America by boat around 600 BC. The Lamanites had been "turned dark" by their turning away from their covenant with God. According to Mormon doctrine, they are the ancestors of all Native Americans — a history contravened by the considerably older archaeological record that surrounded the occupiers of the refuge every which way they turned. The video goes on to show a mind-boggling if also riveting scene in which the leader of the Lamanites is humiliated and actually scalped in front of his own people. Moroni also figures prominently in Book of Mormon episodes in which he stands up to would be tyrants and enemies of freedom among the Nephites themselves. These days he is often imaged in Conan the Barbarian book-cover style, enormously muscled and scantily clad in shining gold armor and helmet, righteously glowering with his personal flag, the Title of Liberty (much displayed at Bundy Ranch in 2014), fanning out behind him. One Mormon commentator on the events at Malheur recalled that when playing as a child all the boys wanted to be Moroni.

A few days later, a figure more widely familiar to Americans visited the land of Malheur to join the Chief Captain, stopping to pose for a photograph that remained — to my eyes — one of the more stunning images of the whole occupation. Though he never revealed his name, given the uniform, the wig, and the imperious stare, it just had to be the Founding Father himself, George Washington — already so well represented in the curious image on the cover of the Constitutional pamphlets poking out of seemingly every shirtfront pocket. Here he was in the flesh — resurrected. Given the circumstances, it only made sense that he'd taken off his civilian clothes and put back on his warrior garb, the full uniform of the Continental Army, to step into the unfolding Now.

I've pulled the picture up again on my screen as I write this. I'm looking at a middle-aged white man in an amazingly well-tailored costume; this thing is custom-made. He's also got a big tricorner hat, white-powdered wig poking out under it. Lots of shiny brass, white gloves, and frilly white shirt-cuffs busting out of the jacket. There's also a sword — enscabbered, strapped to the waist; the hilt is dangling at the belly. There he is in the snow, one foot forward, presenting himself as if for a duel. Behind him stands a white pickup truck and one of the older buildings of the refuge. The sky is gray and there's snow everywhere, so his clothes provide most of the color in the picture. The eye contact he's making with the AP photographer broadcasts a firm, uncompromising nature, as does the tilt of the frown, which seems judicial in its measured but absolute severity. He's carrying a book in his hands. I can't make out what it is but I suspect it to be the sort of text upon which one might swear a binding oath.

¤

Karl Marx addressed revolutionary dress-up a long time ago, in regards to the costume and rhetoric of the ancient world appropriated in the French Revolution and then again in the revolution that brought on the reign of Louis Napoleon. For Marx, it was necessary for the practitioners of bourgeois and reactionary revolution to dress up their relatively prosaic aims in the grand feeling and outfits of times past. Friedrich Nietzsche addressed the same issue when he wrote that the modern European "simply needs a costume; he requires history as a storage room for costumes. To be sure he soon notices that not one fits him very well, so he keeps changing. [...] It is no use. [...] it 'does not look good.'" Poor Nietzsche did not live to see this fine-lookin' fella, but his point is well taken. He goes on, in this same passage from *Beyond Good and Evil*, to give us a little bit of his typically nihilistic hope: "perhaps this is where we shall still discover the realm of our invention, that realm in which we, too, can still be original, say, as parodists of world history and God's buffoons — perhaps, even if nothing else today has any future, our laughter may yet have a future."

And it is true that the laughter bottled up in this AP photograph of militia-inspired cos-play is a richer, harsher laughter than the thin, Bill Maher kind of mirth called up by the prank gifts the internet sent the occupiers (dildos and bags of dick candy) in response to their foolishly worded, widely broadcast plea for "snacks." It's a thicker laughter; it's got wonder and delight in it, as well as incredulity and despair. It's a laughter that laughs at the whole American enterprise, at Walt Whitman's expansive rhapsody reduced to what it has always been at heart — a settler's story, a brutal farce — a map drawn up by white men with guns, to be pinned to the indifferent earth with flags.

¤

But soon Nietzsche's laughter dribbles off into befuddled silence, and now I pick up another image. Here, at my desk, I've got my own copy of the Cleon Skousen-annotated Constitution that poked from every Bundy gang front pocket. It's just come in the mail and the first thing I notice is that the picture of Washington on the cover seems to be an image not of a living body but of a statue — a digitally reproduced or manufactured image of a painting of a statue. And not just a statue, but a wax museum sculpture. The face is a dead mask, the unseeing eyes meet but don't meet mine, while the right hand is permanently stretched out toward me to offer a plume so that I might too become signatory of the great document laid out in the picture's foreground on the table between us, that I might bind myself to it, take the sacred oath.

As I lean back and think about it, I decide it makes sense that it's not the "real" George Washington depicted on the cover, but rather an image of an image. After all, both here and at Malheur, it's not George who's returned, but his dead image that has come to life — as it does constantly in the United States, where his picture on the dollar bursts into speech in so many ads offering everything from mattresses to sound financial advice. (Anthropologist Michael Taussig has written much about this kind of kitschy necro-magic in his work on State Fetishism, work that came to mind for me often during January 2016.) On the back cover of the pamphlet, undead Washington, this unseeing representation of the representation, is also offered to us as a personal witness to our commitment. There is a line where one can sign the following pledge with that proffered plume:

> I, as one of We the People of the United States, affirm that I have read or will read our US Constitution and pledge to maintain and promote the standard of liberty for myself and my posterity, and do hereby attest to that by my signature.

Beneath the signature line is the reproduced signature of a solitary witness — of course, again, it's Washington himself. All the millennia of the witchy European oath magic that grounds the West's fraught relationship to law and language, as Giorgio Agamben and others have persuasively argued, comes pouring through this somnolent mountain of kitsch. Somehow this silliness is also deathly, necro-social seriousness — an oath, no less, witnessed by George Washington, no less. What kind of outcast would the person be who signed this and then turned his back (or her back? are women allowed in this club?) on the true Constitution? Would they lose their true sovereign citizenship forever? Would they find themselves outside the magic circle of (white) American being — sliced off from the We the People Cliven Bundy invokes with such absolute authority in his fiery petitions, to wander, like the Lamanites, unprotected, killable, in the wilderness?

¤

There were other, less spectral visitors to the refuge: day trippers, including local ranchers, came and went by the dozens. In their visits they could learn about the Constitution from Ammon, the rest of his crew, and whatever visiting self-annointed judge or Constitutional scholar happened to be cruising the grounds. Among the vanguard, Ammon's brother Ryan might have been the most insistently militant. He liked to draw a distinction between an inalienable right and a privilege, and there was something Sovereign Citizen about his understanding of the difference. A right needed to be believed in and claimed, he explained to ranchers at the meeting in Crane, or else it lapsed into being an alienable privilege, which could be taken from you. Grazing, he insisted, was a right — deliberately confusing or confused by the language used by the BLM in its administration of a legal good that is

IMAGE: ETHAN COOK, *MONKEY, SQUIRREL AND FRUIT*, 2016, OIL ON CANVAS, 49 1/2 x 38 INCHES.
COURTESY OF THE ARTIST AND ANAT EBGI GALLERY

clearly meant to be alienable — after all, "grazing rights" are for sale. But to listen to Ryan and his brothers, not even the Supreme Court had the right to interpret whether grazing was a right, or what a right was, under the Constitution. No mediating interpretative power was to come between the people and their Constitution.

This gives us maybe the clearest glimpse of what kind of United States they were proposing. What they seemed to want, essentially, was the nation without a federal government, a confederation of individuals, governed by its Constitution alone. The minimal bureaucracy involved in administering the business of this confederation would be left to the county or the state — or "We the People" — depending on whom you were talking to. Kieran Suckling, of the Center for Biological Diversity, long-term adversary of the Bundy war on public land and endangered species protection, told me that, after the Crane meeting, he asked Ammon how he could trust, and how he could guarantee, that whatever county government he proposed to turn over the administration of the lands of the refuge to would be less inept or corrupt than the federal government he despised. "Each time he gave me the same answer," Suckling said: "'the Constitution wouldn't allow it.'" When Suckling followed up by asking what would happen if he and a neighbor interpreted the Constitution differently, Bundy replied that this wouldn't happen either. The document simply said what it said, and would resolve everything.

This was the witchy stuff going down at Apocalypse Ranch. If all this sounds like religion, it's because it probably is — but so, arguably, is run-of-the-mill nationalism. Capitalist economics itself, as Marx so famously pointed out, can be seen as more of a theology than a science. The Bundys are just practicing the fundamentalist, charismatic, revealed religion versions of the state and property fetishism all of us participate in, in some way or another. Maybe this is what makes it all seem so silly, because it's actually quite familiar. (God's buffoons, indeed.) At Malheur, the jubilant atmosphere persisted as if all the occupiers weren't in danger of being carted off to federal prison at any moment — perhaps Ammon had convinced them that the Constitution wouldn't allow it. As Kieran observed, one of the strangest things about the occupation was its mood — how pageant-like it seemed, how endlessly weird and sometimes even fun. Until you remembered all the guns.

Malheur II: "Ours but Not Ours"

AND THEN, SUDDENLY, the Wadatika Band of Paiute Indians appeared (they'd never left) and dragged the whole actual history of the land the Bundys were standing on into the light. Suddenly the boys discovered that the land was chock-full of material refutations of the improvised historical narratives they were offering, and that these literally leaked up everywhere through the dust and the muck, threatening to change the story decisively: they would no longer be liberators of ranch land in the name of oppressed locals and of the holy Constitution, but rather yet another gang of armed and desperate white riff-raff, settlers from outside come to grab whatever they could muscle in on, with some flag-waving and mission-from-God talk as cover for the same old land lust.

Their panicked sequence of responses suggested they felt the urgency of the moment. The attention of the gang turned, morbidly and forensically, to the containment of the physical evidence — the artifacts stored on the refuge — of this return. This kind of containment is impossible in the end — as we all know from our dreams — because the return of the past is continuous; it's an endless arrival. But that didn't stop the gang from trying, digging themselves the proverbial deeper hole, culminating in the colossally ham-fisted move of offering the Paiute the chance to come down and pick up their stuff.

It was the man who had become the occupiers' informal spokesman who took the most active role. Good-natured and drawling, LaVoy Finicum appeared in at least four videos in the last week of his life, including one filmed and posted on the day of his death, that directly addressed the Burns Paiute tribe. In each he pleaded for dialogue, while expressing increasing befuddlement at the tribe's absolute refusal of contact.

His confusion and evident total sincerity can make these videos painful viewing — especially the one that got the most views. Finicum and two other men are seen going through the boxes of artifacts in what looks like a dark basement while Finicum answers questions from the man behind the camera, Blaine Cooper. Finicum starts out by making it clear that the visit to the archive room is a pretext to reach out again to the Paiute, "the rightful owners" — a phrase repeated often in the three-minute video — of the objects in the room. "We're looking for a liaison," he says, "because we want to make sure these things are returned to their rightful owners," before pointing out particular artifacts and beginning to enumerate the wrongs they've suffered. Of immediate importance to Finicum — it clearly seems to him cause for serious outrage — is the rodents' nest he says he's discovered in one box. Cooper interrupts to summarize, saying, "basically the BLM or whoever was in charge of these native artifacts [it was the Fish and Wildlife Service] just kind of boxed 'em up and left 'em to rot down here."

The boys move through the room, checking the artifact tags to confirm that some of the stuff has "just been sitting down here [...] locked away here for nobody but them [the feds] to look at whenever they came down here." Sometimes for as long as 35 years! Finicum reiterates his plea for dialogue, even going so far as to state a willingness to hear about the Paiute claims on the land (claims that Ryan Bundy had dismissed) before the video concludes with another plea, this time from Cooper — a plea that could only have sounded respectful to a group of people hopped up on the sovereignty of private property: "the rightful owners need to come back and claim their belongings." To anyone else it sounds like the Paiute just got evicted from a storage space.

It just wasn't going to be that simple. The boys weren't going to pack up history and hand it off, "respectfully," to the "rightful owners." "It's not just the artifacts," said Tribal Chairperson Charlotte Roderique. "We're in the dirt. Our history and culture is in the soil. We're still in the soil." The problem for the Paiute wasn't so much that there was dirt on the artifacts, or that animals had been in the boxes where they were stored, but that the artifacts were out of the earth at all, and being gone through publicly by a man whose words and actions, despite his constant repetitions of his desire to be respectful, were nowhere near appropriately reverent.

This misunderstanding extends beyond the Bundy gang's relation to the Wadatika — it is the source of the ever-present conflict between Native American people's relation to their ancestral lands and pasts and the discipline of archaeology and the epistemology that underpins it. Tribal archaeologist Diane Teeman explained this to me very frankly, in reference to her own ambivalence about her profession. For Teeman, "It's a community in the dirt. I use that word. And when we dig it's an offense against that community. It's why I became an archaeologist, not so much to participate in this particular knowledge-gathering system of the West, but to minimize the offense that archeology is to these communities in the soil." Teeman recognizes this as a somewhat quixotic position. I was struck by how it was also a very practical one, devoid of any of the absolute, all or nothing, "when will you stand" purity that was to kill Finicum in the end. Archeology is, after all, here to stay for the moment. It has tremendous power over how the meaning and value of lands immeasurably precious to the Wadatika are culturally and legally determined on local and national scales. Teeman sees no choice but to participate and hope that something like what she calls "real collaboration, not just adding an Indian or two to your team" will keep happening, as it has in her tribe's relationship with the Fish and Wildlife Service archaeologist on the Malheur Refuge. She hopes that, as this kind of collaboration increases, it will form part of a larger development of "more robust" transcultural knowledge-gathering practices that might, with changes in laws governing artifacts, eventually lead to some or all of the artifacts stored on the refuge being returned to the dirt communities from whence they came.

¤

In the end, the video did elicit a response, but not the one Finicum and his friends had hoped for. Two days after the video of Finicum in the artifact room was posted, the Burns Paiute wrote a letter to the US attorney general and the FBI urgently demanding action — the video was at the center of this escalation of pressure from the tribe. Tribal Chairperson Roderique cited the historic obligation articulated in the 19th-century US treaty with the Northern Paiute to ensure the prosecution of "any crime or injury [that] is perpetrated by any white man upon the Indians aforesaid […] according to the laws of the United States and the State of Oregon." These clauses, sometimes called "bad men clauses," highlight the complex, deeply ambivalent relationship between Native American tribes and the federal government, one the occupiers didn't seem to understand well — and one that came into play with increasing importance in the ongoing conflict.

¤

The artifact video gets creepier the more I watch it: it's like Finicum is surrounded by so many ghosts that he can't see them. It's like he can't see them because they are everything: they are the air he's breathing, the ground he's walking on; they are what's stored in the boxes stacked on boxes stacked on boxes; seeping from the objects chipped by hand, used, and discarded for millennia by the people known as Paiute and their ancestors. It's the nightmare of the settler, repackaged as Stephen King horror: he's totally surrounded by silent Indians, even if in this case their silence is the silence of the dead. And he can't sense that silence, because he's the one talking, telling his own story about how horrible the dirt and animals, how horrible for the poor artifacts, this sacred property, to sit in a room undisplayed for 30 years — a timeframe with no significance when one considers the near-geologic timescape of native presences and absences. It's like he's in the middle of a ghost dance but he can't hear or feel or see a thing as it slowly turns around him, like he can't see the images that already now are pouring through his flesh.

And then you have to remember that this store of artifacts — wherein the absence of thousands of Native American bodies surface continually toward presence — this is nothing: the ground of Harney Basin he's walking on every day is full of these "belongings." They are buried in the dirt and marsh muck, and just lying on the surface. Nobody will ever be able to come by and pick it all up. You can't just leave history out on the stoop for the "rightful owners" — it's everywhere, it's in everything. He's surrounded by relationship, and he's also in one — one he's not going to be able to dictate the terms of, especially by resorting to discourses of liberty and property. And it's going to kill him. Soon.

¤

I first talked to Jarvis Kennedy a few days after the death of Finicum in the January 26 FBI operation in the Malheur National Forest's Devine Canyon, about 30 miles north of the wildlife refuge. "You know," he said, "we don't think it's a coincidence that he died. No disrespect. We feel for his family. We didn't want that to happen to him. But you can't go messing with objects like that without protection." Kennedy went on to explain some of the rituals of respect and protection he and others in the tribe do when they come upon artifacts: "whenever we find anything […] we bless it, say a prayer, or sing, sprinkle some tobacco or sage on it, and return it to the earth, because it's ours but not ours. I think that's hard for people to understand."

Many explanations of cultural practices I heard during my week in Burns, and in subsequent phone conversations, have been punctuated with variations of this: "I don't know if you can understand that," "it's hard to explain," "it's hard for people to understand." These refrains, usually coming at moments of intense interest for me, moments when I felt very much like I understood and was dying to hear more, have served to remind me to be skeptical of how much I think I do understand — and to remember that no matter what affinity (or envy) I feel for these types of knowledge and ritual practices, I will never have the same kind of access to the temporalities of survivance that these rituals emerge from and open onto. Neither, of course, did Finicum, which is why he was able to imagine that something like a dimension, threaded through the land and through the Paiute, could somehow be boxed up and returned to something called "rightful," something called an "owner." The ontologies of property and sovereignty that sustain white being and that have determined the cultural and economic relations to earth that shape both me and Finicum, however differently, can't be easily wished away either it will take a lot of work, a lot more of the collaboration Diane Teeman talked of, and maybe something more dramatic as well.

When I first asked Diane about her relation to ownership and property, she explained that of course the Paiute historically had no such conception — not in any way that corresponded to the absolute notions of the Bundy gang — and that, for her (and she felt that this was the case for many other Paiutes), the land feels like a relative. "It's a family relationship. Ownership doesn't describe that. You can't own your relative. Everywhere around here, all the dirt I dig up in my garden, my ancestors are woven through that, and that land is woven through me. I don't know if people can understand. It's hard to explain."

In her scholarly work, Diane has touched on the inadequacy of ideas not just of property but also of the sacred to describe the Paiute relationship to landscape. Compared to the vocabulary Diane offers in its stead, the language of God and Law seems both pompous and impoverished. While the typical picture of a "nomadic," "foraging" culture like that of the Northern Paiute might describe their concept of land ownership as nonexistent and their religious practices as "animistic," Diane proposes a different understanding of landscape as a palimpsest of ever-shifting relations — so that, in her words, "an action on a landscape is not only an action on prior acts and events but also the people who were involved in those activities." The old line about walking lightly on the earth acquires added urgency in the context of these words.

It also makes her gardening complex. And not only because the dirt is like a relative, shot through with the material traces of her ancestors. Our conversation turned, at one point, from the dirt to plants and the seasonal gathering cycle. This brought us back to property, sedentary agriculture, and a Wadatika figure I'd been reading about with growing fascination in the Harney County Library Western History Room: Oytes, the Dreamer prophet and shaman from the time of the Malheur Reservation, who had sat beside Egan as he delivered his speech of rebuke to Agent Rinehart. There was no strict catechism for Dreamers, but Oytes was known to have strongly rejected agriculture and with it private property, as the great Dreamer leader of the Columbia Plateau, Smohalla, had done. Smohalla explained to a US army ambassador, who had sought to convince him and his people to take up farming and ownership of individual plots of land in order to become "civilized," that both land ownership and work were prohibited to Dreamers. "Men who work," he said, "cannot dream."

Smohalla explained further that those who violated the earth by owning it or digging deeply in it to cultivate plants for consumption would lose access to the coming world, when the earth was literally overturned. All the native dead would return with this refreshed and plentiful earth, alongside lost populations of animals and plants, as the dream world merged with this one. Diane had her own thoughts about Oytes's principles. "I think I can see what he meant," she said,

> there is something very strange … kind of absurd … about taking one part of the earth and saying only this kind of plant will grow here now, and that this plant's only purpose is to be eaten by me. I've been thinking a lot about food lately in this way. It does totally go against our sense of reverence and reciprocity. It's so important to acknowledge that nothing exists just for me; if we take a plant, or part of a plant, we always make an offering, or ask permission. We need to respect the plant's liberty. Sometimes people nowadays leave coins.

I remembered, with excitement, that I had seen a few coins out earlier in the week, on the sage-covered rims of the lava flows east of the refuge. Later that week — on the Walker River Paiute Reservation in Nevada — I was to see coins in cups placed on the grave of the most famous of the Paiute Dreamers, Wovoka, the prophet of the Ghost Dance of 1890.

Wovoka's ghost dance emerges at a different historical moment than the practices of Smohalla and Oytes; the Bannock War has been lost, at horrifying cost to so many Paiute. The possibility of escaping the white man's regime of property and work has come to seem impossible; there is nowhere to hide, and violent resistance has proved again and again to bring only more terror. Wovoka's messianism proposed a more give-unto-Caesar approach to the white world than Smohalla's. This acceptance of local white wage economies and regimes of property went on in one dimension, while the dance and its trances operated in another, bringing on the return of a renewed earth, and of the native dead. "They are coming," Wovoka said in a letter to Cheyenne visitors. The time was ripe; Jesus, he said (the religion was thoroughly syncretic), had already returned to bring the refreshed earth with him. "He appears like a Cloud," Wovoka said in English to an Arapaho delegate taking dictation at Walker River, "everyone is alive again, I don't know when they'll be here." The new land that was coming would overturn or literally bury the property regimes and political realities of the whites as it arrived with all the resurrected dead — human and animal. The spirit world would be completed and poured out onto the new earth. And finally there would be enough to eat.

¤

The relation of private property to messianic Native American practices, like Wovoka's Ghost Dance and the Dreamer Religion from which it emerged, is often overlooked. The primary narrative of the Ghost Dance focuses on the adaptation of Wovoka's teachings by the Sioux in 1890 — and the subsequent slaughter at Wounded Knee. As such, it is understood in the dominant cultural narrative as a kind of grand and elegant farewell of Native peoples, when actually it seems to have been more of a strategic reinvigoration and key tactic of survivance. Wherever messianic practice has surged up in Native America, the violent imposition of the absolute reign of private property has usually been involved. The struggle that went on between the Paiute tribe and the Malheur occupiers this winter was, on a more politically unconscious level, the continuation of an older struggle. In many ways it was a battle between, on one side, the inheritors of the vast tradition of which the Ghost Dance was one instantiation, keepers of a relationship to land and time that is, at its heart, indifferent to sovereignty, and, on the other side, the cowboy mysticism of sovereignty, property, and violence that coalesced, in this instance, around the Bundy family. In week four of the occupation, it was violence, perhaps the true "title of liberty," that was about to surface, sadly and seemingly inevitably, in its most overt forms.

¤

On January 26, LaVoy Finicum filmed one more plea to the Paiutes and then, joined by Ryan Payne, Ammon and Ryan Bundy, Brian Cavalier, and Shawna Cox, headed up Highway 205 in a pair of trucks toward the snowy, pine-stubbled mountains. This was basically the entire leadership of the occupation — all veterans of Bundy Ranch. Despite the increased surveillance they'd begun receiving from the FBI in the wake of the tribe's letter and the intense pressure from local and state authorities — pressure the earnest and genial Finicum had responded to the previous day with ominous reassertions of his willingness to die — they must have all felt pretty great. This was a potentially momentous occasion. They were on their way to John Day, a mountain town in adjacent Grant County, to a public meeting where they were to speak along with Grant County Sheriff Glenn Palmer, an avowed Constitutionalist who carried the same Skousen Constitution they all did, and had recently even been voted the "Lawman of the Year" by the Constitutional Sheriffs and Peace Officers Association. Even more importantly, Palmer, to the horror of law enforcement, had spoken out against the FBI in favor of the occupiers, just the day before. The possibility of another occupation, and the growth of the revolution that they had been living on the Malheur compound, must have augmented the intensity and excitement of purpose that had so visibly animated their strides since the first drive out to occupy the Refuge on January 2. In John Day, a crowd was already beginning to assemble to hear them speak — but they would never arrive.

For the moment, though, they must have felt great — they were the vanguard of a vanguard, traveling with mission, galvanized by it, through that landscape already so conducive to expansive feeling. The territory they moved through could only have collaborated with their feelings: as they came up over Wright's Point, the basalt and sage of that butte top was bewitched with snow; next, as they crested, the white and gold, salt-blue and green distances of the basin and the highlands sprang open all around them. In a few more minutes they reached the end of 205 where, joining 395, it turned up toward the foothills, winding through snowy fields of golden grass into the mouth of Devine Canyon. It's an intoxicating ride, the kind of drive that makes you want to sing along. It's especially thrilling in the first moments of entering the canyon; as the road curves, and the canyon snakes up and up into the mountains, its chunky basalt walls rise on both sides with the solemn authority of Easter Island heads. As you move, the walls continue to grow around you to the twisting measure of your ascent. It's one of those everyday sublime automative moments the American West is so full of, where the world itself seems to expand to the thrill of your own fossil-fueled momentum.

I took my rides up Devine Canyon under considerably different circumstances, but ones stained with the affect of their ride as I imagined it — and even more deeply infected with what followed shortly after. Especially conscious of the magic borders of federal property, I imagine they must have noticed the sign announcing they were crossing over another invisible line as they burst out of the top of the canyon into deep snow and pine slopes and into federal land again — this time, the Malheur National Forest.

From this point on you can watch it all on YouTube, in the full-length or edited video clips provided by the FBI. In the long version the aerial camera hovers over a line of dark vehicles parked on a forest access road; you can see Finicum's white truck, with the smaller, less visible gold-colored jeep that carried Ammon Bundy and Brian Cavalier just behind it. The line of black trucks begins to pull out of the forest, but the camera has stayed with Finicum, or with his avatar — his truck is really the main character in the film. In 30 minutes it will still be spinning its wheels in the snow while tiny Finicum has already expired, shot down amid his own pleas to be shot, interspersed with demands to see his friend, the Constitutional sheriff. For the last part of the video, he's lying there in the snow with one arm raised like an antenna — I wonder what images his body received with his last breaths. Meanwhile, his truck spins on and on, churning its wheels, still stuck in the deep snowbank to the side of the police barricade he'd tried to run; small figures move in and out of the growing assembly of other trucks as the afternoon turns toward dusk. Some of those tiny people moving around down there are his comrades, being taken in, one by one, with ceremonial slowness, into the body of that vast abstraction — the government they professed so much hatred for, and yet with whose power and violence they had sought an almost religious intimacy.

¤

Death magic and the fetishism of violence was everywhere in the days after Finicum's demise. I arrived in Burns a week after the arrests, and spent a week in the Silver Spur motel, which had already achieved a celebrity of sorts as the motel of choice for the militia. The place was full of militia and media when I got there. An older, affable, if rattled-looking dude, in camo and backwoods beard, smoked and guzzled 32-ounce cups of gas station coffee while muttering to himself on the snowy balcony, fulfilling a certain stereotype of a militia guy. More of these dudes were young, with intense stares, some with cowboy hats, but many with black-hooded sweatshirts. There were a number of women as well, also grim smokers, shivering outside their rooms in the mornings while their trucks defrosted in the lot below them. One woman had even brought her horse. The press bustled about with their own sense of mission. There were at least two documentary filmmakers at the motel. One night, I listened, transfixed, to one who occupied the room next to me while he paced on the balcony telling someone on the phone the story of how he'd been trapped in John Day, waiting to film the meeting the night of the operation that snagged Payne, Cox, and the Bundys, and killed Finicum. He'd had to loop around the mountains to get to the refuge before the FBI arrived. The panic there was wild, he said, he'd gotten some great footage.

The town was especially tense because BJ Soper, of the Pacific Patriot's Network militia, had announced plans for an operation — a "miracle" he called it — for that Saturday, February 6, that would somehow escort the last four occupiers from the refuge, through the cordon of Elite Team FBI Agents that were penning them in. What this plan was nobody ever learned, because on Friday Soper changed plans. Now he asked everyone assembled in Burns or en route to meet for a rally at 1:00 p.m. at the vast improvised memorial that had sprung up at the side of the road on the snowbank where Finicum had been shot. There was a five-foot cross and many flags, including an inevitable confederate one — the kind with an automatic weapon and that slogan from the Alamo on it. A photographer I'd met at the restaurant down by the now closed-off entrance to the refuge had explained how easy it was to find — so, with a few free hours Saturday morning, I decided to go check it out and see what magnitude of death aura was leaking from the roadside shrine. I headed up early that morning, hoping to spend some time alone at the site before the militia converged.

On the drive up though the landscape, my sense of mission increased — as did my pleasure and discomfort with that pleasure. I put on music — Neutral Milk Hotel — it seemed perfectly suited to the redneck (to use a favorite Finicum word) mysticism of the whole Bundy thing and its spermatic patriarchal erotics. "Semen stains the mountain tops" — this phrase was repeating as I moved through the canyon, growing more and more trepidatious as I crossed Poison Creek, approaching where I knew the site had to be. As I emerged out of the top of the canyon into the forest, I recognized the road from the video where the line of FBI vehicles waited. But then something happened — or nothing happened, actually. There was no memorial. I passed out of the National Forest into a

ZACHARY LEENER, *FIVE ETCHINGS (PENTHOUSE)*, 2015, SOFTGROUND, DRYPOINT, SPITBITE, AQUATINT, 16 3/4 x 14 1/4 INCHES, EDITION OF 10 (3 AP), COURTESY OF THE ARTIST AND TIF SIGFRIDS GALLERY LOS ANGELES

wide, high mountain valley, given over to a particularly large-seeming cattle operation: dark shaggy cows traveled in slow elaborate circles through the snow behind big red machines spewing out moist gobs of green and gold shredded hay. I continued on, confused, reentering federal land, more rocky, snow-covered pine forest. After an hour of driving I gave up. I needed to get back to town for a phone meeting with Diane.

¤

In that conversation, Diane explained in depth to me the Paiute concept of puha, a spiritual substance. "Because puha is the power or essence of each person, it's on everything they make or use, so that traditionally we bury people with all their most important possessions, less important stuff is burned — so that none of it can cause harm to the living and so that the part of the soul of the dead that must travel to the Milky Way isn't held back." Diane told me about all the preparations she had to go through in her work as an archeologist, to protect herself from sickness. Her own father had suffered from a mysterious ailment for a long time, traveling to see Western doctors and shamans on various reservations before a shaman at the Bannock Reservation at Fort Hall had a vision of a disturbed grave in a mountain pine grove that her father recognized as one he had passed through before becoming ill. It's because of puha that the tribe was certain Finicum had been placing himself in mortal jeopardy in that video in the artifact room. And because of his own puha and the evident turbulence of his spirit during his time on the refuge, along with the violence of his death, the refuge was now an even more dangerous site, one that would require serious cleansing before tribe members would be comfortable returning.

After talking with Diane, I had a few more hours before meeting Jarvis at a big community dinner for law enforcement in Burns, so despite all I'd just learned about puha, I looked up the exact coordinates of Finicum's death site and set out to try again. I'd seen lots of pickups, festooned with enormous flags, headed north past the motel earlier on — I figured I wouldn't miss it this time. Following the same route, listening to the same music, I felt a new degree of mission now spiked with extra dread as I snaked up Devine Canyon and into the trees.

I was right, this time I couldn't miss it: there they were, and there it was. Where this morning there had been nothing but a bank of roadside snow and its special aura of fatigue, there was now an uncountable sea of flags, and a little wooden cross. There were white people on both sides of the road, some stomping back and forth in the snow, a few raising more flags in a clump of pine, while others paced the road. The woman from the motel rode back and forth on her horse in front of the growing memorial. I recognized many faces from the Silver Spur, but this time they met my eyes with an open hostility that ignited my paranoia about the whole enterprise — this mass bath in the invisible substance that leaks from every site of sudden, violent death. I drove on slowly into that same valley, turned around near the same cows, now huddled in wind-defensive clumps in the snow, and, snaking through the crowd again, headed back down the canyon in silence — dread having drowned out all sense of purpose.

When I got back to the motel, I found out what was up — why all the glares and why I hadn't been able to find the site earlier. In an unexpected confirmation of my feeling that there was a magic war being waged in these parts, I learned that the original shrine had been removed in the night by unknown hands — presumably to thwart the rally at the site of Finicum's martyrdom. News articles were already posted quoting an enraged BJ Soper offering a $500 reward for info about who had done it. He had promised to buy "every American flag in town" and rebuild the memorial. It certainly looked to me that he had.

¤

That night I met Jarvis at the big dinner. He'd been out of town, and, as we still hadn't met in person, I told him what I'd be wearing so he'd recognize me. He texted back: "I kind of stand out in this crowd." And he did. He's at least six feet and three inches, with the build of a lineman, and a ring of feathers falling from his eye tattooed on his cheek — he's a tattoo artist by trade, besides being the current sergeant at arms of the Wadatika Tribal Council. We found each other immediately in the mob scene of white folks in winter gear. An hour-long line circled the enormous hall to get burgers being cooked up by a crew of ranchers in cowboy hats on the biggest grill I'd ever seen, out back in the snow. In the center of the room was the party of Harney County Sheriff David Ward, whom the dinner was honoring, along with the rest of law enforcement that had been involved. Eventually Jarvis and I worked up the courage to get in the line; we had a long time to talk, occasionally interrupted by local folks coming up to thank him again for saying what they hadn't been able to.

As we circled the room, I brought up a story Diane had told me about the repatriation of Egan's head. Members of the tribe had flown to DC to get the eloquent chieftain's skull from the Smithsonian. Many rituals of protection had been required of the delegation, as the skull had undergone much disrespect and mistreatment. I was stuck on images I'd formed in my mind of the delegation sitting at the gate with the skull in some kind of special skull container under the TVs blaring CNN. Or, on the plane, flying over Nebraska, the Dakotas, the Continental Divide with the man's head — was someone allowed to hold him in their lap during take off? Diane reported that many members of the tribe had felt, despite Egan's importance as a hero of the Wadatika, and the fact that he was a blood relative of many in the band, that to bring his disturbed remains back onto the reservation was to invite sickness and calamity. In the end, the repatriation party prevailed. Once back on the reservation, the Wadatika returned Egan's head to the earth, and did rituals and offered blessings to try to bring him peace. This history reminded Jarvis of a moment in January, a prayer gathering in the early days of the Malheur occupation, not far from where Egan's head is buried. Facing east on a hillside, the group had made a number of offerings and prayers for the resolution of the occupation, and sung songs around a fire — until, Jarvis said, they had all begun to feel their numbers grow. The sense he had was that Egan and the other dead had joined them, were standing behind them, in an expanding semi-circle. "You felt it, right?" he asked an already nodding companion.

This reminded me of Russell Thornton's demographic revitalization argument about the Ghost Dance. Thornton makes the case that, as the self-understandings of Native American groups changed, and their numbers decreased, the need for the political presence of the dead grew. He argues that participation in the Ghost Dance was related to crucial demographic revivals among many groups on the verge of dying out. I asked Jarvis if that companioning sensation of warriors backing up the small circle assembled on the hill that January night had felt like a kind of ghost dance to him. He said, while he doesn't think much about Wovoka generally, he had found himself thinking of the Ghost Dance prophet in the intense days of the occupation. "Maybe he was thinking about this time," he speculated, "maybe he saw this conflict. My own father always told me another battle was coming someday and that me and my brothers should be ready." We fell silent for a moment; slowly we circled the whole room on our way to the grilled meat.

If it was a kind of war, and Jarvis told me later it had felt like a war to him, it seemed to me that it was being fought at the strange confluence of politics and magic, where power and feeling are gathered into bodies, as bodies are gathered in feeling. In the end, the Paiute had clearly been better prepared for this kind of warfare than their opponents. With their ghosts came the earth itself, and that earth sustained and supplied their ghosts. This earth was the very earth the occupiers stood on, earth they had no understanding of except insofar as it held potential economic value — fuel for cows — for their imagined rancher constituency. Really, they had known nothing about what they were getting into, they had no idea where they were — something that became painfully evident in the cell-phone video of Shawna Cox, shot from inside LaVoy Finicum's truck after it was pulled over by the FBI. Finicum had admitted his total ignorance of the landscape in an earlier interview. He said when he arrived at the refuge on January 2 that it was the first time he had ever been there, but he'd seen a bald eagle taking off from a fence post as he hurtled down 205 and taken it as a sign that this was the place.

¤

I also saw an eagle on a fence post, on my way out of town the next day. And I was thinking of Finicum too, headed back down 205 one last time. I had decided to take the long way home, around Steens Mountain, out to the Alvord Desert, and down the back way to Winnemucca, Nevada. I felt an imaginary line running through me as I drove — the line they'd traversed that last day — running in reverse, north to south from the National Forest to the Refuge, between the new sacred site of the militia, where Finicum had expired in the snow next to the churning wheels of his truck, and the ancient sacred earth of the Paiute where, if you listened to the tribe, Finicum had contracted his fate.

Up again I went, over Wright's Point; again the basin unfurled beneath me, running out toward snowy Steens to the south. I stopped again at the closed entrance to the refuge, and tried to eat again at the restaurant at the Narrows (great chicken fried steak), but after an hour and a half of waiting I had to split: they were swamped, this time with FBI agents at least 25 of them. This was a totally other collection of white-man energy: neatly trimmed beards, pre-weathered baseball caps, nicely fitted jeans and t-shirts — and each one in a different stylish windbreaker or light-weight zip-up wool or leather jacket. Where did they all shop? Mostly they were talking about the upcoming Super Bowl, when they weren't trading stories about various kinds of manly recreational equipment. I bought some hard-boiled eggs and nuts and shoveled them into my face in the car, pulling out onto the refuge at an unguarded point a few miles down the road, where I climbed a butte up through the sagebrush to get a last look at the marshes, the pastures, and the lakes.

When I first met them, I'd asked both Diane and Jarvis what it felt like to spend time on the land of the refuge, with the knowledge of that sublime persistence of their people in that landscape. Diane had said that, whenever she is walking on the land, as she often does in her life and work, everywhere she looks she sees obsidian shavings or even objects, the whole basin is full of them. "Everywhere I go I feel accompanied," she said. "In this landscape I never feel alone." "Oh man," Jarvis had said, "just go down there to the refuge. You'll feel it when you get there. You'll just see them there … you'll see the people in their winter villages, all the wickiups, smoke rising from the fires, people in reed boats fishing on the lakes."

I had found on each visit out to the basin that it was as Jarvis had said — I could see them there, moving among the reeds, smoke coming from the wickiups that themselves looked like big clumps of sage. Maybe reed boats nosing through the reeds on the lakes. Sentimentally, I began to imagine the voices of children, as I thought also about something Charlotte had told me, about learning as a child to make baskets of the tule that grew here — baskets for egg gathering. She was taught to whip one together in a few minutes right there in the marshes. She was also taught by her grandmother that, when she found a nest of eggs, she could only take one if there were at least three; she had to leave one for the birds, one for the coyotes, and then if there was one extra she could take it. While looking out over the lakes and finding it surprisingly easy to picture the scene Jarvis had suggested, I also noted how different that landscape would be to me if I had, like Charlotte, been taught to weave baskets of the reeds that grew there. It would be a different experience if I had often gone stepping quietly through the marshes in search of those nests with at least three eggs, and if I had done it under the tutelage of a grandmother who reminded me that little girls like myself had done the same for thousands of years, right here, where I walked.

Later, hiking along the sweeping volcanic ridges of the Diamond Craters lava flow area to the east of the refuge, weaving took on a more metaphorical register for me. As I walked, with increasing deliberation and attention through all that distance, omnipresent snow-blown Steens Mountain popped up out of the rolling sage desert to the south like a slumped beast. It seemed to have its back to me — or was that just the rolling indifference of its ongoing face? Fetishist that I am, every mountain in the desert seems to me, at some point, to be an impossible head, a planted skull, dense with all that implausible time coalesced as rock interior: the inorganic mind, a secret brain of solid space. I know this fetishism to be ridiculous and solipsistic, but it also holds a place for the mountain beyond whatever I could ever experience of it through the limits of my body. I guess I want to believe that my fetishism brackets its autonomy, its liberty, as Diane says about the plants. In this way I can imagine its thereness as something totally without me.

It's possible that this makes me not all that different from the fetishists who occupied the refuge — instead of the Constitution, I had the absence or the presence of the mountain, a transcendent power so deep in the world it's outside the world, presiding with an indifference beyond sovereignty, over my fantasy ritual of weaving myself into vanishment. Because I felt that's what I was doing, weaving myself away. Straight ahead to the west, the lakes of the refuge and its swaying grasslands and marshes fanned out, while to my right rose the snowy foothills and mountains where tiny video Finicum had leapt from his truck and met his white sovereign fate in the violent arms of the law.

Moving through that big western silence, as my posture improved with the deliberation and attentiveness of my stride, it seemed I could be reeds woven into space, that the walking was a weaving of myself as movement into that landscape, so that eventually, if I walked with the proper care and reverence, on the other side of it, the thing called I, a simple strand of material in the wind, would be finally, truly pulled through. Then only landscape and distance would be left, there where I was not: in the magic basket of my vanishment.

Of course, the problem is that I still seem to be here — right now, for example, with you; I'm no more gone than the day I was born. Maybe this was the ultimate problem for Finicum — that there is no way out of this palimpsest of relation — culture, society, history, whatever — without a final leap into death: maybe death is what he meant, in the end, by freedom. The last chapter of Finicum's novel, *Only By Blood and Suffering*, is actually called "Freedom." The book ends with the death of its hero.

I got back in my car and headed south toward and around Steens. As I was crossing a pass to the west of the mountain, I startled a big herd of antelope. They ran from the road to a safe distance and then turned and stared back while I stood next to my car. It grew windless, mad quiet for a moment, and I could hear my nerves singing in my flesh as the antelope and I faced off for a few seconds, before they turned their heads back to grazing.

An hour or so later I arrived at the Alvord Desert, around the other side of the mountain, where I leapt from the car and ran out onto the hard, sun-cracked playa — the waxy cake of the lake floor. I ran. I turned around. I turned again. There was Steens, to the west and north now, and to the east a hard ring of shimmering blue buttes. I imagined walking straight out into it forever as I began to do some more "weaving," walking on the baked land with eyes closed into the sun, now above Steens, with slow and then slower deliberation, and then stopping in one of the deeper creases of silence. The wind was gone again. The sun was on my eyelids; it was gold here in the dark; my eyeballs felt cradled in the glowing folds of their lids. The humming of my body was back, it was a thick yellow buzz now. I pictured "me" as an outline traced by the bodies of bees and opened my eyes again to see Steens — looking down right at me — right through me, and away.

¤

Back in California, when I next spoke with Jarvis on the phone, I was eager to ask him about the power of Steens that I felt I had experienced so intensely on my last day in its field. I don't really know what kind of answer I expected, but it was different from the answer I got. He said, about the mountain, "I just see them up there, our people, camped out, hunting, gathering. They are up there. So the power is not any different from any other place for me. We were everywhere, you know. We might've been on Steens on Thursday, but who knows where we'll be tomorrow." Here was land as family again, an entirely different kind of fetishism from my own. I wanted the mountain as some kind of heteronymous force — with enough attractive power in its field to pull my insides out, and turn me into a ring of bees or weave me into space. Jarvis needed something else — something calmer and bigger than what I needed. What can I do, I am in love with the desert, for better or for worse. He just wanted to be there, with them, and he was.

"Hey," he continued, "I got something for your *article*." It turned out that he and Charlotte and some others had gone out to the refuge that week — the FBI had invited the tribe to be the first civilians back onto it. They hadn't been allowed to get too close to the crime scenes, but they'd gone up on a slope by the now iconic fire-watch tower that had been converted into a sniper post during the occupation. And they'd built a little pit and a fire and done smudging with sage of all who were present, including a few curious FBI agents. I wish I'd witnessed the tribe blessing the federal men of violence who, at least this time, had lived up to the obligations in all the broken federal treaties Charlotte had cited to protect Indians from the incursions and abuses of bad white men. "We prayed for their families and for their safe passage home, and we prayed for Finicum and his family too — you know we didn't want that to happen." And they blessed the refuge, he said. "And I sang a song." "What kind of song?" I asked. "A victory song," he chuckled. "You know, it was like I said in the beginning at the news conference. We were here before you got here, we'll be here when you're gone." ❖

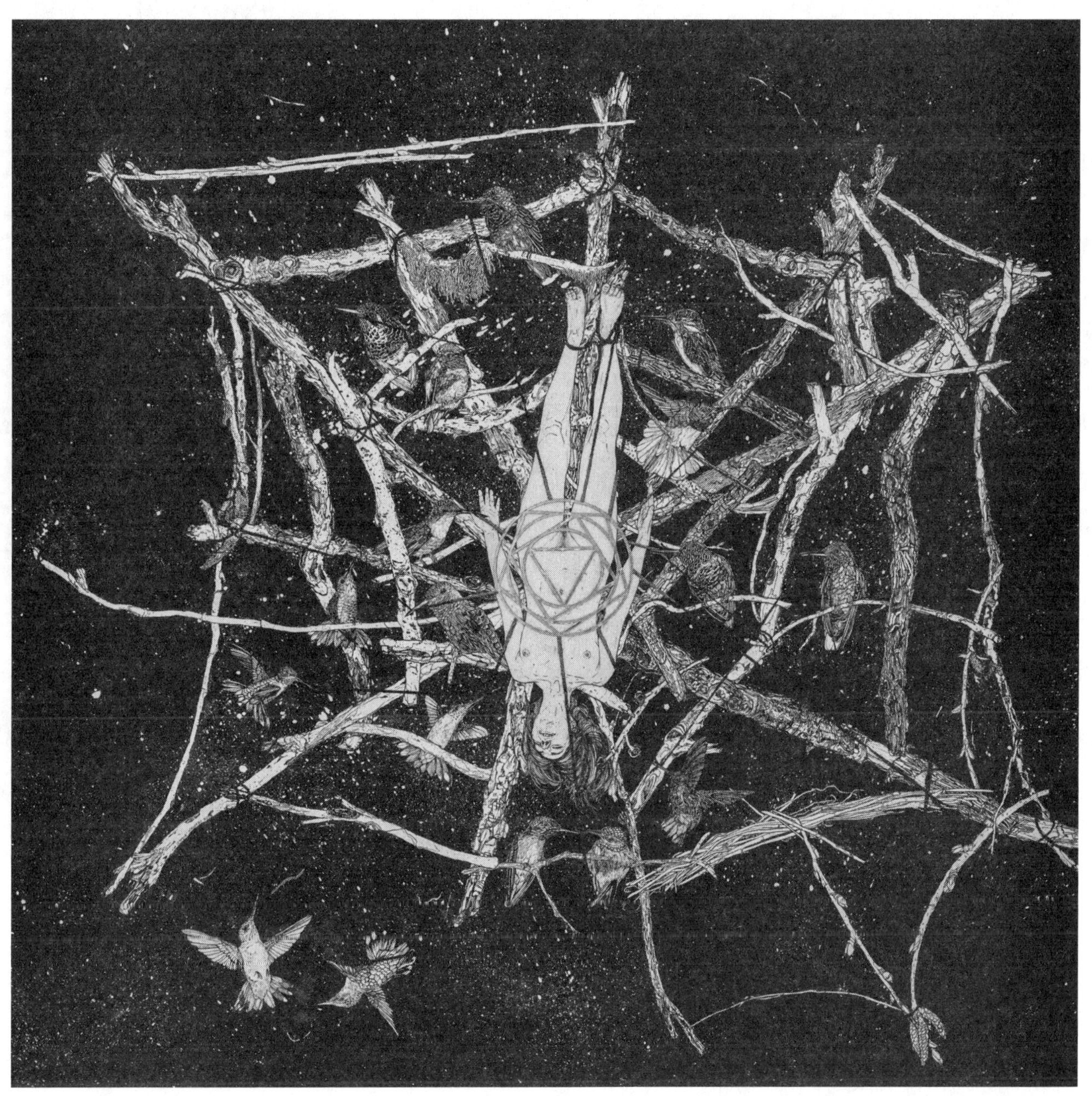

KYMIA NAWABI, *DREAM CATCHERS*, 2016, GLITTER, HAND-CUT IRIDESCENT STICKER AND INK ON PAPER, 24 x 24 INCHES. TO VIEW MORE OF KYMIA NAWABI'S WORKS PLEASE VISIT HTTP://WWW.KYMIANAWABI.COM

Archeophonics

PETER GIZZI

I'm just visiting this voice
I'm just visiting the molecular structures
  that say what I am saying
I am just visiting the world at this moment
  and it's on fire
It's always been on fire

I'm saying this and it's saying me
That's how it works, seesaw-like
The archive in the mouth and the archive is on fire
That's the story
The sun and the body and the body in the sun

It was like this just like this
The world that's coming toward me
And the world around me
Around me are words saying this
  saying fire
Saying something or all of it

The World Is Not Conclusion

PETER GIZZI

When I look out your window I see another window
I see a wedding in my brain, a stylus and a groove
a voice waving there

When I look out your window I see another window
these trees are not real they grow out of air
they fell like dust they fell

So singing is seeing and vision is music
I saw diadems and crowns, daisies and bees, ribbons, robins,
  and disks of snow
sprung effects in pencil-light

When I look out your window I see another window
I see a fire and a girl, crimson hair and hazel eyes
a public in the sky

When the world comes back it will be recorded sound
that cooing shrub will be known as dickinson
the syllabic, fricative, percussive, and phatic will tear open

Out your window I see another window
I see a funeral in the air I see alabaster space
I read circumference there

Night Work

Peter Gizzi

The eyes take their relief in dark
in this night room seeing things.

The waking dark old-like
a monk's pagoda in some far bell country never seen.

To have never seen it in me ringing
the night room the gone steps creaking ens.

To remain like this
what the world wants.

The motor fumbles in the distance
anything becomes rhythm in the distant wave.

You can ride it if you can hear it
the whine of night the ongoing ribbon.

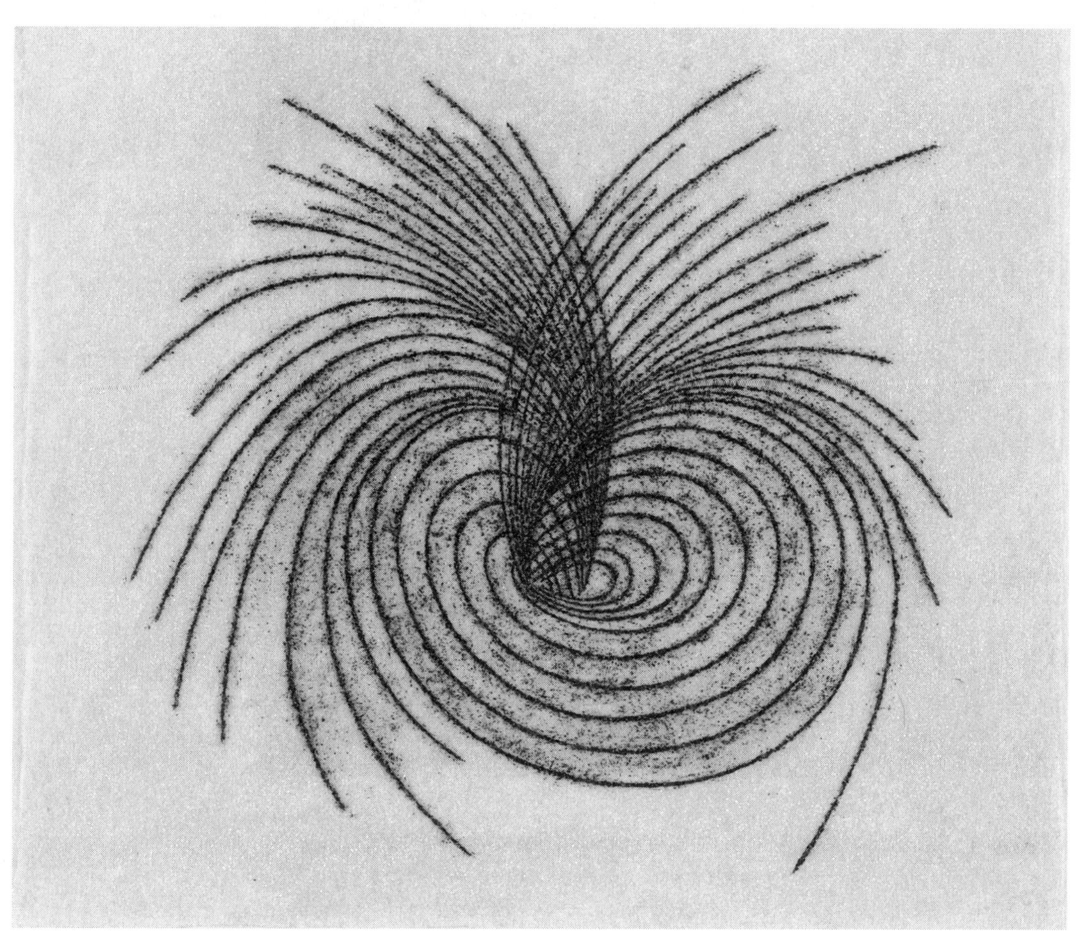

CHERIE RACITI, *BLACK HOLE #1*, 2013, ACRYLIC AND FIBERGLASS 17 x 19 INCHES FRAMED.

Tattoo (Inspired by the Tattooed Lady)

A COLLABORATIVE ESSAY BY LEE GULYAS AND BRENDA MILLER

MAUD STEVENS WAGNER, TATTOO ARTIST CIRCA 1907

LEE

AT FIRST, you read everything you can: advice columns, etiquette manuals, cookbooks, the classics, anything to help you become "the perfect woman." You cross your legs, take piano lessons, write thank-you notes, learn to apply makeup — not too much, just enough to highlight your natural beauty.

Next, you practice housekeeping, scrubbing and folding and ironing, and when you are at school or in line at the pharmacy or the grocery store with your mom, you scan the faces of the women, and you notice they look nothing like the faces on those checkout-stand magazine covers. They look nothing like the women on TV.

You realize that no matter what you master, it will never be enough — you can always be prettier, smarter, richer, nicer. You never wanted to be nice.

You want to be as strong as the deep green of a cedar forest, as free as the rain on your skin and so you rip your tights, wear boots and cut-off t-shirts, and learn how to apply makeup from the drag queens next door. You quit trying to be perfect, and start finding your way back into the light of yourself, into who you were before you entered the narrow canyon of rules and limits, and you forget about decorum and smiling, and stop. You stop until you trust yourself again. You cut off your hair and wear as much fucking eyeliner as you please, as you please, and you don't look back, not from guilt or shame or regret, no apologies, no misgivings or self-reproach; you don't look back.

¤

Brenda

THE WOMAN who serves me my Moroccan mocha has a heart tattooed over her heart. Not a Valentine heart, but an anatomical organ — with its muscled chambers, its arteries twining up her neck. It's hard not to stare as she bustles behind the counter, slides my coffee toward me, makes my change. She has bleached blonde hair and wears a yellow camisole. Tattoos run up and down her arms, and two silver rings pierce her nostrils. Her voice is tender as she asks me how my morning is going.

My morning is going fine. I'll be drinking my mocha at a window spotted with late summer rain. I'll immerse myself in the din from the tables surrounding me. The voices seem to be speaking in foreign dialects; I can't understand a word, but get all the meanings from gestures, the way friends lean toward one another and laugh. Or the way they bring their hands, folded, toward their mouths. Someone reads a book, her eyes flicking up at intervals. Someone crochets a scarf. Several people work on computers or gaze into their phones, scrolling and scrolling, waiting for messages.

There's no discernable narrative, nothing that tells a story. It's all image, flashes of memory; perhaps you can see the outline of a knife, hidden among ordinary kitchen implements, or the black handle of a gun against a river. But it's so confused, this pattern that keeps shifting the more you try to study it. Better to look away, drink your coffee, keep your gaze on a life that unfolds just on the other side of the window.

I live a life untroubled, yet trouble often rises in my heart nonetheless. It's not the kind of difficulty one can talk about, even among good friends. And yet sometimes it feels tattooed in a visible place: my forehead, perhaps, or cuffed around my eyes like spectacles. Or maybe it's a full-body sleeve, continuous, peeking out from the hem of skirt, blooming from my collarbones. The colors are muted: remnants of rose and olive, bits of gold here and there, a little bit of blue. ❖

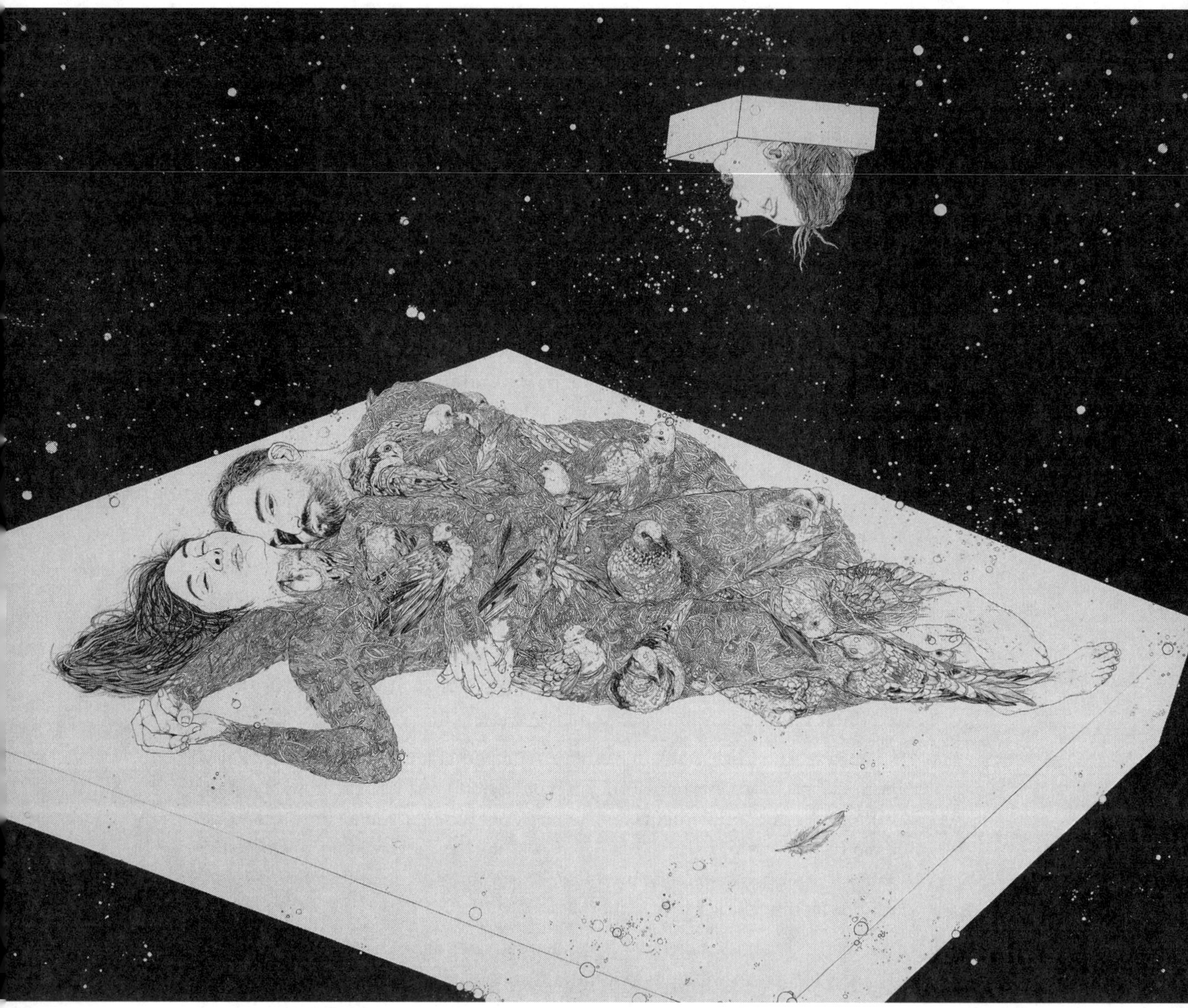

KYMIA NAWABI, *THE FUTURE*, 2014, ACRYLIC AND INK ON PAPER, 24 x 30 INCHES. TO VIEW MORE OF KYMIA NAWABI'S WORKS PLEASE VISIT HTTP://WWW.KYMIANAWABI.COM

Pluto

AZAREEN VAN DER VLIET OLOOMI

THERE ARE TIMES when I think my life must have begun with a No.

I take this thought, which is also a feeling, with me everywhere I go. It is nestled somewhere deep in the grooves of my past. There are people who notice I carry around this ancient negation. They become curious the way I have seen certain adults become curious about wild animals that are about to go extinct. How terrible to know that a creature that has been there all along, suddenly, on the verge of its disappearance, becomes visible. I allow these people to approach me, but I don't always answer their questions. I pick and choose. Over the years I have become more deliberate in my ways. If I tell an overly constructed person about my negation, they become uncomfortable. I interpret their discomfort to mean that their own void has suddenly become palpable to them; their gaze turns glassy, they detach. They look disturbing to me then, their eyes vacuous as if they have been unplugged from the world.

When I get restless, I go out into the woods, or I walk down the path along the swiftly moving river. I imagine the river's water has sprung from the navel of time and, therefore, like time, to be continuous in its flow. I picture the river carrying its load into the future, into the future's future, into the unexpected beyond to which I will never arrive because my life will have been extinguished. I don't account for droughts and erosions, or for large-scale geological changes that will affect the river. It comforts me to think of it as ongoing.

Halfway down the river path there is a store with organic goods called The Purple Porch, where my husband and I spend a great deal of our time. There is nothing purple about the store and there is no porch, but the produce is excellent. Everything on offer feels pure, plucked from the source. The clients have a clean aura about them. They appear to have reached a state of total clarity, final and static, that is forbidden to me. I watch them drift through the well-lighted aisles of the store. They seem to possess the ability to levitate. It doesn't matter how high the shelves are stacked, everything is within reach. Sometimes, I feel the urge to stand on one of the wooden lunch tables and announce to the clientele that eliminating mixed emotions from the repertoire of their lives — like exhilaration followed by the anticipation of defeat, or joy mired by the sudden remembrance of mortality — not only flattens their experiential dynamics, but may also cause others, like myself, to perceive them as unreal. I go to the store despite my better judgment. Despite the fact that going causes me to slide down a mental rabbit hole at the end of which I arrive at the bleak and horrifying conclusion that these people are passing the burden of managing the dark radiance of their personal void onto future generations, their children and their children's children, who are bound to drink from the waters of their orphaned grief. This, I believe, is how our identities become confused with one another. And because I see the self as a mosaic of mirrors, I believe we are all reflecting back to the world not only own our joys and turbulences, but also those of the people who have shepherded and interfered with our growth.

A young woman who pins her curly black hair to her scalp with beaded, silver butterflies, or plastic hibiscus flowers that catch the pink of her cheeks, works at the counter. She is incongruous with the rest of the crowd who wear simple cotton clothes and who have natural silver hair they rarely brush. When my husband and I go to the store together this young, bejeweled woman raises her voice. She doesn't do this when I go to the store alone. The amplification of her voice is something she reserves exclusively for my husband, who, I have to say, handles her treatment rather exquisitely. She doesn't seem to understand that volume will not complete his command of the English language. She doesn't seem to understand that he is not hard of hearing. She once screamed that his credit card doesn't work. A cluster of round faces turned to look at us — for a second they looked to me like a row of white pills — and then averted their gaze and resumed their meal. This simple gesture of bringing the cutlery to their mouths reestablished their humanness. The young woman irritates us in more ways than one. For example, she asks us whether or not we are members of the co-op regardless of the frequency of our visits. If we pay for our coffees and sit down to drink them and then get up a few minutes later to buy a baked good, she will ask us again.

It is Saturday and we are at the co-op. When we sit down with our food my husband tells me he is going to wear a sign around his neck the next time he comes into the store. He has had it with her. He is at his wit's end.

"What will your sign say?" I ask.

"It will say: No, I am not."

I tell him I am that sign, that I believe I emit a vibration that resembles the sound of that No. He looks at me intrigued, then carries on with his meal. The gesture of resuming one's meal must be a coping mechanism people employ in awkward situations. I once read somewhere that food triggers the same pleasure centers in the brain as sex, that eating has the capacity to restore a sense of well-being for the person who is trying their best, but failing to manage a delicate situation. Reading the article, I also learned that bragging about one's accomplishments awakens the same pleasure centers, joining food and sex to form a triangular elixir. I have not provided my husband with the emotional context out of which my comment has sprung as naturally as water from a fountain, so I don't blame him for being confused. Unsure of what to say, he offers me a piece of corn bread. He offers me some of his coconut soup. He is trying to be helpful, but my void, I want to tell him, feeds on abstractions and is less satisfied by material objects like corn bread and soup.

I get up and walk to the restroom. It turns out this is where the purple has been hiding all along. I stand there, staring at the walls as if it were a horizon to behold. Someone, presumably one of the cooks, has affixed cooking pots of various sizes to the walls. The pots aren't arranged in any particular order. I look at them from every possible angle, directly and then through the mirror above the sink. For a second, I get distracted and look at my face. I don't recognize it. I feel a palpable estrangement, which makes me think that somewhere along the line of my life I must have registered a distortion that obscures my perception, an atmospheric disturbance that persists. I look at the pots again. In the mirror's reflective surface the pots' round, aluminum bases shine with redoubled force. The discs blur into a single moon, the walls retreat. I am left standing in a mauve desert, washing my hands at a sink in the silver glow of a fake moon. When I look at myself in the mirror again recognition doesn't appear, but a memory does: a photograph of Pluto's magnificent dark disk backlit by its sun. I looked at the photograph in the morning, the distant planet with its friendly heart immense and beautiful.

I want to tell my husband: there is so much I don't understand. But something gets in my way. Instead, I tell him about the pots and pans in the bathroom; I point out an oven, used as street-side decor, into which someone has stuffed tomato plants and removed the burners and grates to allow the stems through; I draw his attention to green beans that have been threaded together and attached to clothes hangers and left to twirl in the parking lot.

"Do you think the world is in good enough health," I ask, "that we can afford to create art out of food?"

I am always asking him impossible questions, to which he responds with the same aloof, intrigued look I have seen on his face when he confronts crossword puzzles during long flights across the Atlantic Ocean that, because of their length, send me into the upper echelons of paranoia and him into a focused meditation on words.

We leave the co-op and head south on our bikes to the farmer's market. Everything we own in this town used to belong to someone else. We purchased our bikes for a dollar each at an auction a few doors down from our house. Our neighbor died suddenly and left behind half a century's worth of objects. It was my first time at an auction. I had no idea what I was doing, or why I was doing it, but once I had started I couldn't stop. I found everything at the auction to be of the highest entertainment value. I watched a bald man wearing a muddied wifebeater purchase an old, dented blue-and-white telephone company sign for $450. After that, he acquired a green dentist's lamp that had been rusting for decades, old dentures, a child's football shoes from the '50s, a remote controlled truck. I had my heart set on a pair of binoculars. By the time they were being auctioned, it was evening. I was still standing. I had been there since eight in the morning. I had skipped lunch. Food seemed to pale in comparison to this magnificent event that had manifested on our otherwise dull block. A man with wisps of white hair and missing teeth and whose fingers were stained yellow with nicotine wanted the binoculars I was set on winning. "No way," I told him (I grow bold when I'm weary the way some people do when they're drunk), "I've been waiting around for those all day." He brought his bloated yellow hand to his chest and pounded it to release his voice, which he swiftly employed to order the auctioneer to slow down in case I wouldn't be able to "keep up with the speed of things around here."

Because I know the ways of language, I felt optimistic about my chances of achieving my goal. Soon his stabs at me would attract an audience for which he would have to perform. I played along. I fanned my face. I massaged my back. I made myself appear fragile, breakable. He told the others to look. He told them he believed I belonged at an art auction where things are executed with a great deal of pomp and gravity. My prediction was coming true. People were bemused. They gathered around him, nodded along. What else were they going to do? He had built a story out of nothing and, like desire, once it was there, it was a reality that had to be accounted for.

Later on at home I stood behind the window and stared out through the binoculars. I had won them. I felt victorious. I bragged to my husband. Endorphins coursed through my body, confirming the theory of the triangle of elixir. I searched my surroundings. I was thrilled to inspect the world one section at a time, to see it up close. This sudden shift in perspective led me to again think of Pluto, of how access to the planet had revolutionized our understanding of the universe. In my mind's eye, I drew a line from Pluto to the deep, undiscovered wells of the self where our memories are stored. It occurred to me that if a memory were to surface after having been repressed, it could radically shift our perception of the self — the way Pluto had shifted our perception of the cosmos. And because some memories awaken earthquakes in the architecture of our being, it occurred to me that a Richter scale could be used to help us more effectively communicate with our loved ones about the extent of the damage and the scope of the shift our personal landscape endures during each memory-episode. I wondered if this could help others understand each "new" us more clearly. I moved the binoculars around. Straight ahead, I saw a red cardinal inspect a branch on our sycamore. I looked up: a giant cluster of clouds rushed by, ushered by the rising wind. Then, lower down on Earth, a man with a plump red face leaned against our gate, loosened his tie, smoked a cigar.

At some point my husband came around and said, "Don't get into the habit of spying on people!" He said this as if spying were a contagious disease I could suddenly catch and subsequently have to submit to, rearranging all my other habits to give utmost priority to this newly acquired one.

I pointed the binoculars at him. He put his arms up. He said, "Hey, don't shoot the messenger!" It was unclear to me who had sent him to deliver the warning, to sound out the black trumpets of war.

At the farmer's market, my husband and I walk through the booths talking about the green beans, which he has, suddenly, half an hour later, taken an interest in. I interrupt our conversation when I spot a necklace at a booth that reminds me of someone I have loved deeply in life, but whose presence I have felt too troubled by to bear. I walk over to look at the necklace more closely. I am ready to purchase it, but then I remember that we have used all our cash. I explain this to the vendor. She shrugs her shoulders, wraps up the necklace, and puts it in my hand. When I feel its weight, I suddenly decide I no longer want to own it. But it's too late, because she has closed my hand around the necklace, and said, with mystical overtones, "Claudette trusts you to pay her another day."

¤

I am weary, exhausted from holding my void. But I don't want to put it down. There are people I care for who want me to extinguish my negation with no consideration for its roots. I am what I am, I tell them; I can't change where I come from. I say this to them in the hopes that they will understand what they are asking me for: to endure the world as not myself. I tell them that I have inherited certain storms I believe I have to weather. I tell them that we can try all we want, but that there is no avoiding the long, exasperating hike through the wound of history we have been creating since time immemorial.

Thunder and lightning have imprisoned my husband and me in our house for a week. Tornado warnings have sent us into our damp, unfinished basement. We light candles. We pass the time drinking whiskey, laughing, playing cards, comforting our dogs who nervously pace the darkness because they are uncertain of its boundaries. When the sun returns a week later, I ask my husband if he would like to go out onto the river with me. We head out to the Dowagiac. We launch our used kayak. The creek is high from all the rain. It moves quickly.

I have never lived somewhere where life has been so compartmentalized, neighborhoods so segregated. We plunge our oars into the rough waters. We navigate around logs and rocks over which the water rushes. Downstream, the water is slightly calmer. There, we encounter families who glide past us in rubber tubes. The adults are smoking cigarettes, drinking cans of beer. The children follow suit, screaming with excitement. Everyone here is white. We can't seem to find places that reflect the rich demographics of this town we live in. This failure saddens and confuses us both, because we know we are inhabiting an erasure that perpetuates a great deal of abstract harm that carries with it severe material consequences that lead, in turn, to more abstract harm.

We row toward an island and drag our kayak out of the water to rest. We climb into it, lean back, and stick our faces in the sun. My husband plunges his hands into the shallows. The water is incredibly transparent. The sand at the bottom is full of cliffs and grooves and shines like gold in the shimmering light of the day.

"Touch the sand," he gently orders. He tells me it's the softest surface he has ever touched.

I agree. I tell him it's the softest surface I have ever touched.

He hands me a sealed shell.

He says, "Look, each side is a perfect mirror of the other."

I inspect the shell. It's true. It has beautiful green ridges on both sides and each line is equidistant from the other. Then he hands me a soggy log. He tells me to smell it. I smell it. It smells like a potato that has been left to rot in a bowl of water. I like it when he announces each detail that captures his attention with the fanatic precision of an accountant. A dragonfly lands on my oar. I don't tell him about it. I feel selfish about my silence, but I am worried that breaking it will cause the dragonfly to disappear from view.

Further down the river we come across a campground. It is the largest production I have ever seen. There are canopies, grills, raised decks decorated with living room sofas and coffee tables. The campers are huge. Dogs come barking out of them; they sniff at the meat set out on the grills. A family exits the river. In the process, they lose one of their tubes. A couple camping on the riverbank finds this lone tube drifting downriver to be hilarious. They have been sitting in their Adirondacks for too long. They pop olives into their mouths in between laughs. This pair has brought their lawn decor with them. Behind them, a pale blue flag featuring an exotic bird and the words, "Forget the cracker, Holly wants a cocktail!" flaps in the breeze. They have brought other objects: a water pump, a hammock, a faded statue of a black man in overalls holding a lantern.

I feel a cold draft approach from a faraway place. I feel myself clogging through the deep, dark trenches of history. This is why I like to keep my void close, because otherwise there is the risk of forgetting. I stop paddling. I feel weak, as if the blood has suddenly drained from my limbs. I remember: months earlier I had asked someone I knew if she could recommend a doctor. Her response came flooding back: "I know an amazing doctor, but I have to tell you: He is black." I asked her why that was something she felt compelled to warn me about. She told me it was because she had been raised in this town and had encountered a number of people who were surprised she had recommended him and who had made it very clear to her that they preferred to go to white doctors. You mean racist people? I wanted to ask, but instead I said, I'm not from around here, and tried to close the conversation.

Later on, in my car, I thought what I had said had not been the right thing to say, because it implied that I may have felt differently if I had been raised in this town and even though I could never know what I would feel had I been someone else, I felt a physiological rejection toward the possibility that brought on a sudden vertigo. I was feeling that same vertigo in the kayak now, that same disorientation.

The first time I went to the doctor's office, I saw his nurse practitioner — a plump, white woman with tiny blue eyes, a sharp nose, and a very British sounding name. On my way out she said, "Your next appointment will be with the doctor. That's him right there." She pointed at a series of portraits on the back wall and told me that he was the one in the center. She was preparing me, the way the person who had recommended the doctor had. I stood there not knowing what to say, thinking, on the one hand, of all the violent potential of language, and on the other of the same violent potential in language's deliberate absence, until the nurse, closing the door behind me, ushered me out of the office.

A month later, I saw the doctor. His job was to inspect my uterus and my breasts — to make sure I had remained in good health since my last exam in another city a year ago. During the exam he asked me about my cycle. I told him that my cycle was regular, but that often, in the days leading up to it, I can't sleep and I feel as though I am submerged in water. "Like a fish in a murky aquarium," I said. I told him that during those days I perceive everything through that haze, that sometimes I get lost driving home from work even though it isn't a long drive and I do it on autopilot on all the other days of the month. The doctor is a good listener, and since this is such a rare quality to come by, I was not able to regulate myself well. I told him about the No I was born with. When I finished telling him, he said, "Are you sure this is living, walking around with the weight of all that emptiness inside you?" I told him that I believed it was, that I believed I was living a very full emotional life and that the only thing that bothered me was that here, in this town, I felt alone in my habit of subjecting myself and life to a degree of scrutiny others seemed to avoid. At some point during the conversation the doctor asked me, "What are you afraid of?" This question of his paused for a moment the reckless noise of the universe. I reflected. When I had gathered my thoughts, I told him I was afraid of letting go of the wreckage only to wake up later in life wondering what else I had muted, dispossessed myself of, deliberately erased for the sake of others and the machine of efficiency in which our lives are mired. "I understand," he said. He instructed me to close my eyes and told me to imagine my fear as a wave. He told me that if I look at the wave long enough, it will appear smaller and become more manageable. Then he said: "You are in optimum physical health," and I left content, thinking only of those words: optimum physical health.

The end of the river is drawing near. We navigate our way beneath a low, concrete bridge and then a wooden one that has fallen out of use and is overgrown with grass, weeds. We steer carefully between logs. We float through narrow passes between stones. The creek is an obstacle course. When we finally drag the kayak out of the water we sit on the rocks, silent, tired — together, but each of us alone, and both suddenly exhausted and uncertain as to how it is we should live in this world.

¤

The next day, I go to the regular grocery store to pick up some fruits and vegetables. An advertisement has been painted onto the building's side-wall. It reads: LEATHER BANANA. Someone has painted a giant, ripe banana next to the words. Underneath the banana, an arrow points out to the road. There is no indication as to what the arrow or the banana are referring to, but I am learning to take things as they come. Sometimes I have the impression that this place is a riddle I am not meant to resolve, that all I am meant to do here is observe and carry on. But then I remember that observing is never harmless and that it will change the place in ways I cannot foresee or control. I wonder if instead of the emotional distancing required for detached observation, I should work harder at finding my way into this world. For a brief moment, I feel hopeful that the life I am living in this town will become legible to me and that I will learn how to pass through it without doing more harm.

On the way out of the store, I imagine this town as a burrow. The image is as vivid as a dream; it is detailed and hyper-real. The burrow is made of dark stones that have been covered by ivy and moss. I walk around it. The surrounding land is rocky and arid and I can't reconcile its bleakness with the vivid green covering the burrow. I walk around the burrow clockwise, counterclockwise. I can't find the entrance. I can't find a side, or backdoor through which I can be let in. I think about how it might take a long time for that door to reveal itself and then I remember something a friend who had once been a monk, but who left his community because he had fallen in love with another monk, had said to me at a dinner: "In the monastic tradition, it is considered wise to wait 10 years before passing judgment, or making a sweeping life decision." I wonder if I can walk around this burrow for 10 years. My friend the monk now lives with the man he fell in love with in a house on a hill at the edge of town. During the same conversation, he told me with great affection, "I don't know what I'll do if I have to survive another winter in this place closed in with those cats of ours!" It was the dead of winter then and we had not been able to go outside for weeks. The region had been in a state of emergency. Our dogs' paws would freeze when we tried to let them outside. We sat by the fireplace. We drank whiskey. Our dogs curled up next to us. With every passing day I had felt more resolved to submit to the winter, to surrender to the snow that kept on falling, to the glacial temperatures, the thickening ice. I felt as though the world were pointing all its arrows at the icy grooves of our hearts, as if the winter were relentless in its effort to lock us in and expose us to each other, to ourselves. I wondered if the town would grow as a result.

That night, on our way home from dinner we saw our neighbor standing in his front yard knee-deep in the snow. He was in his pajamas. He had a weathered, distant look in eyes. It was as if emerging from his home after the long retreat the winter had forced on us was for him equivalent to emerging from his mother's womb. He looked haggard, uncertain, vulnerable, and yet possessed all the curiosity he would need to survive in the world. He was holding a measuring stick, which he kept plunging into the snow at various spots across his front lawn, the sidewalk, the street. He was trying to determine the exact height of the event that had hemmed him in and which would soon enough run down the road like the waters of birth do when we are born.

When I return home, I put the fruits and vegetables away and sit down at my computer to look at images of Pluto. I have been doing this every day for a week now. It is a compulsion. I learn that weather has been detected in Pluto's atmosphere, a haze that has the scientists and the space physicists startled. They are enamored with the great sandy heart on its glacial surface that is saluting us from the outer layers of the cosmos. I write down certain things the physicists are saying: "crossing to the far side and looking back"; "a light surrounding the dark disk of the planet"; and, my personal favorite, "how different these objects are despite their closeness in space." I think of the ancient gap that divides humans from other humans despite sharing a life, a town, a room — a gap we are so often afraid of, prefer not to acknowledge, that we refuse to hold.

In the evening, I go out for cocktails with my friends. Along the course of the conversation we arrive at the subject of therapy. They ask me why I go. I tell them I go because I want to be awake to myself. They like this and seem curious about exploring the possibility of their own awareness. I keep going. I tell my friends that I think of therapy as an infinite exploration, as if the self, rather than the cosmos, were the last frontier, and I am navigating its dark and radiant waters. I tell them my theory about the self as a mosaic of mirrors. I tell them I am trying to organize the shards, to get a sense of whose presence is contained in which parts. My friends ask me if I will ever stop what they refer to by the end of the evening as "my investigation." No, I tell them. I tell them that each time I come across a new shard I didn't know was there, I have to go back to the beginning in order to integrate my findings and that this requires me to recalibrate what I thought I knew. I explain to them that each thing that enters my conscious knowledge takes its position next to the others causing a shift in the map, in the geography of the self that is as vast, infinite, and elastic as outer space. I tell them there will be no final shard, because each day we acquire new ones that take their place next to the old ones, creating an infinite regress of mirrors, multiple sets of labyrinthine corridors that have no beginning and no end.

The next day my husband and I go to the beach. The end of summer is approaching. We sit on a lawn overlooking the lake. We are here to watch the sunset and this grassy spot above the railroad tracks and the sandy shore offers us the best view. The sky is a bright, flamingo pink and the sun descends through it slowly. It shifts the sky's color spectrum as it approaches the horizon. The sky turns orange, purple, lilac, and then green. It is every color and no color at once.

I think of my negation. I think of how it, too, is everything and nothing at once, of how it is so large and silent that it is capable of holding even more of the everything that will soon turn into nothing with the passing of the clock.

An Amtrak train pulls into the station. The conductor climbs out of his window and down a ladder that is attached to the car. I have the impression that this image is rushing at me from the past, a distant memory resurfacing to claim its position in the day. A man from the station café greets the conductor. He hands him a coffee. They salute one another. Moments later, the train departs.

Directly behind us on the lawn, there is a restored cannon from the Civil War. It has been put there as a memorial. A man lifts his daughter, who is a toddler, and shoves her small body into the mouth of the cannon. She sits there happily, her weaponized face sticking out of the cannon. The sunset is nearly over. The sun sinks into the lake and disappears from view. A bugle call emanates from the station café, signaling the end of the day, the fall of the sun. I feel myself standing at the edge of my void, peering into the abyss. I turn to my husband. I want to tell him, but don't yet know how, that I feel myself entering a savage dimension, where I am content to be uncertain, happy for doubt to bc thc only thing I know. I hcar thc sound of thc trumpets echo in the distance.

"Ah," my husband says, "another day has set. Tomorrow we will have to carry on." ❖

Song of the Andoumboulou: 150

Nathaniel Mackey

Sophia was Ahdja's twin again, doffed her
Safronia mask. She dropped her presidential
campaign, called it cosmetics, a dream she
wrest-
ed her way from inside. . . Again we stood
outside, again we openly looked, sunlight's
amenable dress our jurisdiction, light's
legis-
lative élan. The schooled men's mystical
politics were not lost on her, the schooled
women's also not lost, nod academy, nod's
elec-
toral draw. . . Heads of tunes lay scattered,
her and hers, everyone's and everyone. Outside
she wagged her finger under all our noses,
"Don't think I don't know." There was no way
we
could drain the moment we knew, no way
drink deeply enough. The twinning and the un-
twinning made us wonder. What was it she
want-
ed us to know she knew we wondered, pretending, no matter we wondered, we knew. . .
Sweet Sophia, lips noncommital, eyelids low,
donned an away look, beginning to be beyond
us
we could see. Thus the case in point of bod-
ily abatement B had become, brother she'd
allow, lover no more. . . So the song went at
least
and we as well. The law's late initiates, sentiment, seminarian affect, feckless word of
late our word of choice. "Don't think I don't
know."

She said it again. "Sweet Sophia," we yelled
out, "what it is. . ." A spiritist banality ran thru
it or if not ran lay in wait, banality and banality's
re-

buke run as one, ran or if not ran lay as one. There
was a place around the bend, we'd heard, the
body would never end. So the hope went and we
as

well, so the song, Dread Lakes reconnoiter's
re-

joinder, Lake Pred's law re-
buffed

•

Sophia, we believed, had taken flight, lost in
the grove our grooved outlanding made us
mock, premature elders it seemed. The academy
of

caw we called it. Crow we called it, owls that
we were, declared we were, each the wise one
the horn sang about, Trane's reed's insinuative
de-

cree. . . Lost in sound we eventually were, heads
of tunes on the ground all around us, lost
country what would've been hers had she run,
ours

only to lick our wounds in, wise though we
were we thought. Brother B, who'd have been her
running mate, retreated, twin to what intrigue
nei-

ther he nor she knew. . . Still he dreamt it, cupped
hands canvassing the hang of each other's hips,
soft second body, soft other side, soft landing politics
had

been when as he dreamt it, wide world their wide
hips and thighs intimated, all in their palms he dreamt. . .
We the chorusing crows cawed, raw recruits, love's
late converts, owls we'd have otherwise been. We
sat

watching it all on TV, stuck to our seats, glass
grove the grove we looked at or looked in on, glass-
eyed, it seemed, ourselves. Hourglass girth one
got
one's arms around stalked us, taunt song's dream
equivalent, his and her compliant midriff, his
and her concupiscent mesh. . . We made our way,
we
lost it, long since gone, we grew ghostly, never
to be heard from again nor not heard about, the we
we
were alluding to alluded
to again

For the few to whom it mattered we wore
white. We wore white, we wore beads
around our necks, we got ready. *Filosofía*
Cari-
beña, Volume One came on the box, *Vol-*
ume Two, we were told, someday to follow. . .
It was long since no longer about Sophia,
simi-
lar sound in proximity, stubborn was what
it was. Not to be forgotten, she donned
her Sofrita mask, no matter the Plumb Choir
we
were tantamount to. . . A soothing song let's
call it,
cool it, we said, Wagogo we'd secretly be

•

A coded way of saying something else it
would've been, the coded way they came
to be themselves. We've all got lives I told
my-
self, I knew she was no one's witness, "Don't
think I don't know" no matter. . . We were
what lay scattered, slapped heads waylaid,
way
head we called it, the way the head lay hurt
after Trane had hold of it. A strain of pique
newly known to us, a straw someone hung
from
broke. "Come Juneteenth," we heard her
announce, "I'm cutting lightweights loose. . ."
Muleteenth I'd have liked her to say but I
heard it still. We've each got a life I reminded
my-
self. It wasn't me nor was it mine to say I saw
clearly, way head that I was, though I was.
And so it went, one slap followed another, one
fin-
ger wagged in our faces more than one, way
head's arrival each one. . . Strewn we lay without
legs again. The Synecdochic Stash Qu'ahttet
ser-
enaded us, "Don't think I don't know" trans-
posed. So it was or so it seemed or so we took
it, go-head entanglement ours to recollect, stairs
had
we had our legs back. . . All the star locations
came to meet us. We were live at the Pershing,
live at Pep's. We've each got a life they seemed intent on repeating. We were live at the Blackhawk,
live
at Ronnie Scott's. . . Live at New Morning, we
were live at Birdland, live at Marty's on the
Hill. Let your grip go loose they seemed intent on
in-

sisting, live at the Lighthouse, live at the Both/And,
  live as the rotted grain we sat sipping, done-dead
An-
doumboulou alive
again

•

Ahdja, Safronia, Sophia and Sofrita each
thought the day was hers, qu'ahttet entanglement it fell to us to address, dreamt assault
by
who did what with whom. Beset by dread,
a message whose mix we drew back from,
wisdom's run for office put away not to rest,
wo-
manly grace we'd've died for, sophic deliv-
erance's day. . . Errant club we could feel our
heads hit by, erotic wish reciprocal mesh
were true polity, wisdom's run for auspice it
was
we wanted, each to've been either, either
all. So it was we fell away stung by wisdom's
visit, sweet idiocy's appeal's broken buzz
out
all around us, tej bet ambivalence's bequest. . .
Wise though we were, sweet idiots, not to
be denied we so knew it, so stout the beat of
blood
we were on. Heady, lightheaded, headed elsewhere, sweet the rapport we dreamed await-
ed us, sweet such release there'd be. Sophic
pros-
pect. Qu'ahttet polity. Qu'ahttet's fore day keep. . .
So it was and so went our run we saw, so it
was or so it seemed. *So* was ever the quick one,
it
the inevitable next, *so it* the coin or the bill we
bought time with. The *so* club hit us incessantly,
soon-come causality on us no sooner we knew,
live
at the So Club had we been the band we'd be. . .
Arms bound by *so* though they were, we were no
band
yet, reach though we did or try
reaching

(slogan)

As it had all been a hoax, a joke, the woo-
ing, the presidential run, *so* so worked
and wrought it was only what was real we
want-
ed, fall back utopic nor dystopic, neither
one, only what lay, stood or sat of its own
accord, unforced, awaiting what made no
pitch,
claim, com-
plaint

Alphabet

M. J. Iuppa

The quick brown fox jumped over the lazy dog became my measured mantra as I drew each letter in glossy black ink, using an italic fountain pen with a stylized left-handed nib. To err, just shy of the end of the sentence, set me back in the perfection of a composition book's page. *O, God help me* (That's nine-year-old blasphemy), *will I be able to wiggle my way out of this?* We were forbidden to tear out pages. A ripped page from the front left, its partner fluttering loose in the back and exposing my inability to be as peerless as my right-handed peers who finished their penmanship lessons in time for chocolate milk and saltine crackers. Not I. I was making up a story about the brown fox with letters that also jumped, leaving blobs of ink that would smear on the heel of my palm. A mess. The lazy dog sprawled all over my page. But I had a small brown bottle of ink eradicator. Definitely contraband, but my sister Karen had shown me how it worked miracles and I knew it would save me. A drop of the liquid drawn lightly with the glass wand over a blob, or smear, or warped letter would lift the ink. Daub twice with a square of green blotting paper — gone. *What are you doing?* A voice that knew full well I was hiding the evidence. *What fox? What dog?* How many times did I start over? It took me years to make it right in a world of quick and lazy letters.

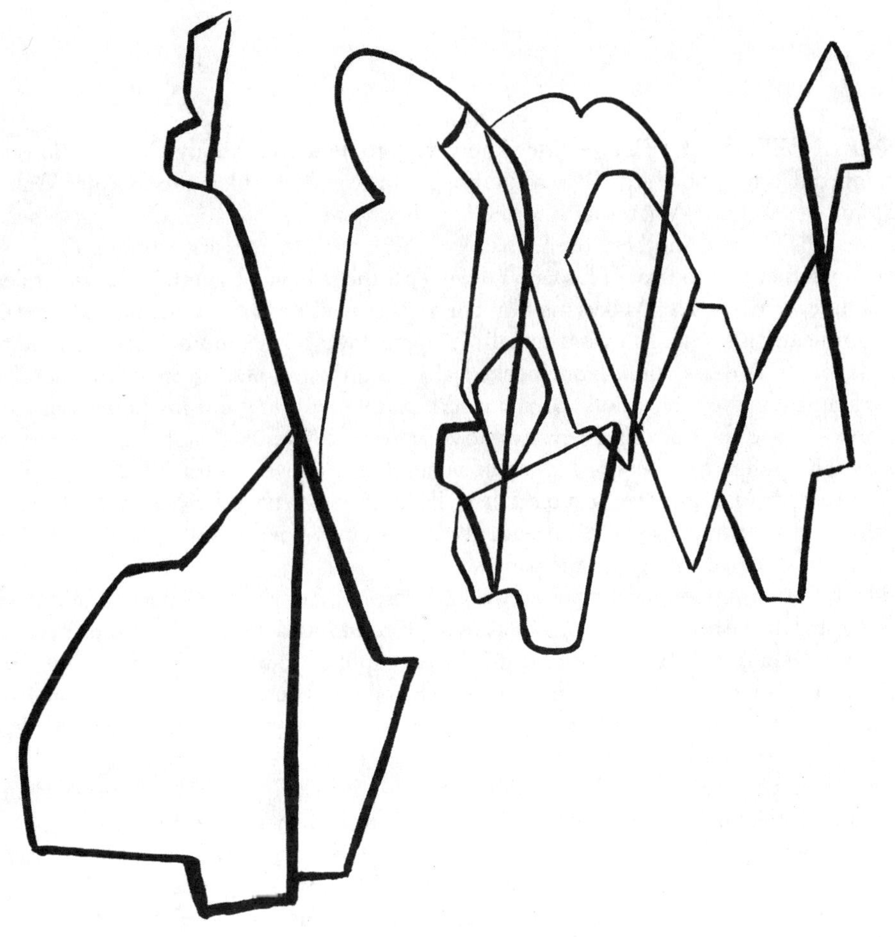

ELISE CAVANNA SEEDS, *VERTICAL PROCESSION*, C. 1942, INK ON PAPER, 11 X 9 1/2 INCHES, PHOTO: MARTIN A. FOLB, PHD. FROM *EMERGING FROM THE SHADOWS* (SCHIFFER PUBLISHING).

North South East West

Nancy Jooyoun Kim

WHEN OUR FATHER DIED, we didn't know what to do with his body. Conversations with your estranged dad never include: "What kind of coffin would you like? Steel? Pine? Walnut?" "How about cremation?" "Where would you like to be *spread*?"

He was 66. He and his best friend had gone hiking. On the drive home, for reasons unknown, my father lost control of his car and went off the side of a mountain. Cause of death: "multiple blunt force injuries." Makes me think of ninjas (or Vikings) just cinematically whaling on him, pummeling his body. But what actually happened was less glamorous, more frightening and mundane. He and his friend got knocked around and smashed up in a Chrysler Town & Country minivan. No man wants to go out like that — certainly not my father, who loved Charles Bronson and felt a stronger devotion to a carton of cigarettes than to his own children.

The local Korean newspaper ran a photo of a mangled vehicle (the same car I had learned to drive in) and a body on a stretcher in a black bag. The nearly one-page article included a picture of my father and a separate one of his friend. We had no idea how they'd obtained the photos, but there he was. He had made into the papers.

Suddenly, he was no longer my father, whom I despised; he was the subject of a tragedy, a story that either left the reader grateful to be alive or plunged into a despair about the uncertainty of life. He was no longer the man whom I, at 23, hadn't spoken to in months. He was no longer the father who had abandoned my mother, my sister, and me when I was six. He was no longer that tall, thin figure with the downturned mouth, the dentures and the metal-filled teeth, the sad brown eyes, the angry lines around his brow, the sagging jowls.

He was just an older man, a father, who went to church, loved hiking, and died in an accident. Just another sad tale that you read in the paper, and thank god that it wasn't you or anyone you know. But, in this case, it was us. It was our sad story. It was our father for whom I had over and over again, through the years, imagined many endings, partially as a form of wishful thinking — after all, that's the way it is, isn't it? That's how you deal with those feelings that make you angry and ashamed. You picture the subject of those feelings being bludgeoned by Vikings and crude weaponry — one of those sticks with the spiked ball swinging off the end of it, or the axe handle with those chain thingees.

Because that makes more sense than real life.

¤

My father was one of those men of a certain generation who seemed perpetually broken — an old Maytag dishwasher in a sea of stainless steel. He was like Willy Loman, except he was Korean American and it was the 1980s, which may have heightened his alienation and despair — all that hairspray and neon everywhere and all he wanted to do was go home, loosen his tie, smoke a pack of Marlboro Lights, and silently sweat.

He had an accent that encompassed the evolutionary, seven-layer dip of inner city Los Angeles: part Chinese, part Brooklyn Jewish, part African American. Yet he was none of those things. When he yelled at us, he sounded like something out of a Scorsese film, but he couldn't say the letter "L."

And he would greet black men in a parking lot with "What's up, brutha," which often resulted in a confounded look on "brutha's" face. As a child, I would just silently recoil from my father as we walked past his brother. *How embarrassing!* But I remember feeling a bit of pride, too, mixed in with the shame. Here was my dad, attempting to bridge cultural gaps in the most awkward, possibly offensive way (maybe not as bad as braiding his silky hair into cornrows), yet something about his naïveté seemed refreshing. Like, in a perfect world, they would be brothers, except that in this actual world black brother was usually stereotyped pointing a gun at your face, and yellow brother cowered behind the counter doing math problems.

He owned, I think, three golf clubs.

He never wore t-shirts, only collared button-downs.

Hence, he had many undershirts.

¤

I hadn't spoken to him since spring, probably when I told him that I had been accepted to grad school in Seattle. And my mother hadn't seen him in years. But being his only family in the States, we had to pick up his belongings from the Los Angeles coroner's office: a fanny pack filled with snacks and maps, a wallet with about $40, and an LG cell phone that still worked.

At first, we didn't know what to do with these objects. But being a practical, immigrant, single-parent family, we went to a Chinese restaurant in Koreatown for lunch and spent the cash.

We were hungry. The hours since discovering my dad's death had gone by at a frantic pace, saturated with decisions and indecisions, alternating between extremes of feeling and absolute numbness. It had begun when my mother and I, sitting in our living room, heard shouting, yelling outside the gate of our front yard. We looked into the darkness and saw the wife of one of my father's friends, not the friend who had died, but another, a friend who had planned to go hiking with my father that day but changed his mind.

With her elderly mother in tow, she'd arrived to tell us, screaming, that our father had died. I'm not sure why she didn't call — perhaps she just didn't remember our number, but she knew where we lived: in the same house as before my father had left us.

They came inside. The agony in our living room was at a fever pitch. Korean women sure know how to crank up the misery, wailing as if their insides were being pecked at and pulled. Here were these strangers of the present, once friends of the past. We hadn't seen them in over 15 years. Here they were in our living room, of which we were ashamed — the old, stained furniture; the cracked ceilings and walls; the dirty paint. Here they were, amid the evidence of our ruin after my father left us. Here they were crying and sitting on our floor.

As we sat there together, I remember the shock that took hold of me as I thought of my father going off the side of the mountain. Over and over I tried to imagine what that must've been like, what he must've seen, felt, or thought.

It was perhaps one of the very few instances in my life when I allowed myself to see the world through his eyes. Mostly, I had hated him for as long as I could remember, for how he treated and spoke to my mother, to us. Yet, as a human being, as his daughter, how could I not feel something for his story, the seemingly endless litany of hardships and failures in his life? From the hours he'd worked standing behind counters in some of the most dangerous parts of town to the final mediocrity of selling cleaning supplies at a small, increasingly irrelevant store in the Valley. His experiences with racism. His foreignness (that accent). His inability to create a family. To love a family. To even feel a part of the family he was born into, with his father in South Korea and his mother and siblings somewhere in North Korea, separated from him forever when he was only a child, and escaping the war.

And finally his death — the pain, the suffering, the violence, the loss of control.

Everything — the living room, the world — zoomed out for me at that moment: it was as if I were staring at a distance at my mother, my father's friend's wife, her old mother with her crown of gray hair, all of them crying, sitting on the floor in a very Korean way, heads hanging, napkins for wiping their eyes and noses crinkled in their hands. I realized that, from an artist's or writer's perspective, this was a touching, even beautiful scene. I wanted to be the one to write it. At that moment, I thought about what a monster I was, thinking of writing, thinking of beauty as these people suffered before me. Ugly and self-serving, I know, but it's the truth. All I could think about was art.

¤

My father immigrated to Los Angeles in the 1960s on a student visa for a PhD program. He already had his bachelor's and master's in economics. He came from a well-educated family: my grandfather, his father, was a lawyer, and later a judge.

Growing up, I never understood why my father moved to the United States. He seemed to have more opportunities in Korea than here, with his lack of language skills and the fact that his degrees from Korean schools meant nothing in this country. Eventually he dropped out of his PhD program, and then spent some time working in factories, before owning small businesses, from a gas station to an army surplus store to a women's clothing shop. Like most immigrants, he had a tough life with the primary challenge of supporting this family, and the secondary challenge of having some sort of identity — both within this country and within the self.

As he struggled with the physical realities of our lives, the limitations of what we could have, how much money he could make, how far he could go, as an immigrant, as a person of color, without family or the credibility of an American degree, I believe that secondary challenge, conceiving who he could become in the absence of fulfilling his dream, destroyed him.

He drank a lot. He reeked of tobacco, of whiskey. When drunk, he would sometimes lie nearly comatose on the couch, or slurring and playful. He was almost better that way, because, when sober, he was more likely to fly off the handle, to scream and yell and shame.

In addition to his sadness, his rage, his disappointment with life in America, my father also expressed a strong and strange level of disdain for Korea. He thought it antiquated, boring.

He didn't like the formality. He did like American food and movies. The clothes and glamour. The guns. His strongest ideas about this country and what it should be came from the movies — the ones starring actors like John Wayne and Charles Bronson — films that were not only a breeding ground for unrealistic expectations, but also for misogynistic and racist beliefs.

My father's American dream, perhaps similar to that of other immigrants, was basically to become a white man. Not that he literally wanted to look into the mirror and see a white face staring back at him — or maybe he did. Of course all his heroes were white: all the images of power and glamour — all the things he wanted and didn't have — belonged to white people. White people, as far as he was concerned, were always the protagonists, the stars of meaningful, triumphant lives. Even I, an American child born in Los Angeles in the 1980s, didn't want to see my own small eyes, my own face. I wanted to see, I don't know, Christie Brinkley?

So my father's disdain for his homeland, and his desire to escape and reinvent himself are easy to understand, especially if you have an idea of what it was like for many Koreans from the north, who had been split from their families while fleeing for the south, prior to and during the war that would eventually divide thousands of years of culture and blood and language and love in two.

Along with his father, he had fled the north, leaving behind his mother, who was ill, and his siblings, with the plan of returning for them one day. Hundreds of thousands of Koreans had done the same, traveling through miserable conditions. (Today, seeing images of Syrian and Eritrean refugees flooding the shores of nearby countries, with sometimes nothing more than a backpack, if anything at all, just relieved to have what is left of their family near them dismantles me, not just on a personal, familial level, but on a level that reaches inside the organs, the bones. It is clear that although home, nationality, and culture inform our identity, nothing sustains, nothing keeps us alive more than the desire to keep our loved ones safe, to keep them from pain.)

My mother who had fled the north at age four, would tell me and my sister of the dead people she had seen along the roads, the families who had clung to the tops of packed trains, desperate to get out, only to fall to their deaths in the tunnels. She was "lucky" in the sense that most of her immediate family made it out, but my father, who was maybe 12 or 13 at the time, would never see his mother and his sisters and brother again. It was just him and his father now.

How could any of them have imagined that a border would divide them for the rest of their lives? How could anyone have predicted the horror that is now Korea, the horror of being hacked in two? How could we have seen the state that country is in now: how ludicrous, how insane, how utterly devastating?

North Korea may be a punch line to some — with its comically narcissistic dictator, inept missiles, loud fax machines, and generally high level of cultural tackiness — but to us, people whose families live beyond the barbed wire, that division, between us and them, is a source of deep pain and shame. How did we make it out without them? How could we have left them behind? What happened to them? Do they wonder about us? Or have they died off? And are we already forgotten?

There is no way to comprehend this trauma, except to zoom out from or turn off the screen.

And it's easy, it must be, to despise the people that reattach us somehow. Maybe that's what my sister, my mother, and I unknowingly did to my father. We were reminders of the loss that he had worked so hard to bury and run from, and forget forever in a tangle of work, alcohol, and rage. We were reminders of what he could not control, of the arbitrariness of his survival. How could he reconcile day-to-day life with the deaths of those he had left behind, or with the fact that perhaps, somewhere north of the 38th parallel, his family might still be alive?

When my father eventually left my mother and sister and me, perhaps he was reenacting that other escape. He was creating his own borders, his own DMZ.

¤

We decided to do a joint funeral with the family of the friend who had also died in the accident. I don't remember who suggested this. Odd as it was to collaborate with them — we hadn't known each other well when the men were alive — a combined ceremony would ease the burden of decision making and honor a friendship that had lasted decades. It seemed like a good idea from both a symbolic and practical point of view.

Unlike the other family, we opted for cremation. We decided we would throw the ashes into the ocean. We remembered our father taking us to the beach when we were very young, before he left us. It made sense to send him back to that vast body of water, that metaphor for the unknown, plus we couldn't afford a plot for his grave. We'd never had much money — my father never paid child support — and yet now we were responsible for his remains. My mother couldn't stop complaining about how, in spite of his cruelty and absence, he'd left us with the burden of his final care. We had to buy him a coffin for the funeral showing and, when we went to the parlor to look at the caskets, which were absurdly displayed in miniature, like little hamster coffins, we had to choose the cheapest one.

It was plain and made out of the dullest wood.

I went to my father's apartment to pick up clothes for him to wear. It's an odd thing going into a dead person's home, especially when you have not seen that person in a very long time. The whole place seems so quiet, and it's as if you must respect that by keeping your voice low.

But who is there to hear you?

¤

My father left us in 1987, a week before my sister's 10th birthday.

I remember coming home from school to our three-bedroom house in mid-city Los Angeles and finding that most of our furniture was gone, as if we had been robbed, ransacked for all the heavy things — all that solid wood — of our lives.

But, it was my father, not a stranger, who had somehow felt entitled — who had taken the furniture and run. It's hard to say what the logic was there. Perhaps, as the primary breadwinner, he felt he'd earned that dining room set, that coffee table, the queen-sized bed that he'd stopped sharing with my mother a long time ago.

Anyway — there was a note taped above the living room thermostat, maybe 15 or so feet away from the front door. I remember my mother reading the note, as she cried and crumpled to the floor. A deep knowing overcame me as I realized our life had changed forever. I don't have any distinct memory of what my sister was doing at this moment. Maybe she realized, too — or maybe she was wondering if my father would ever return.

¤

Before the funeral, we approached the viewing room and saw the two open caskets and my father and his friend inside, looking like dolls, their faces painted to cover the bruises, the gashes. It was the first time I'd seen a dead body — and there he was, my father, wooden and waxy — his hands folded in front of him, one on top of the other in white gloves. He wore the red tie that I had chosen for him and a crisp black suit.

Someone complained because we had requested closed caskets. The funeral people swiftly apologized and shut the lids.

The other family had spared no expense on the coffin, gleaming and white like a Cadillac, or the large color photo of their father surrounded by flowers. We ourselves only had a humble eight-by-10-inch in a simple black frame with a black ribbon tied around it. I felt incredibly sad for my dad and for us; for the lack of money in our wallets and love in our hearts. He and we were poor in every way possible, it seemed.

During the service I cried more than anyone else in my family. I held the tissue box in my hands, wiped my eyes, blew my nose the entire time, bent over, sobbing. I couldn't stop and I didn't know why. My mother and sister cried, too, but for whatever reason, I couldn't contain myself. Was it the sight of that casket so simple and plain? Was it the grief of the family across the aisle? Was it the surprising number of people who had shown up for us? People whom I had never met, members of his church in the Valley who had made the trek to be there? Was it my father's sadness that made me cry? Or was it all my own?

¤

I don't know what my father did after he left us, where and how far he went.

Less than a year later, he came back to visit. By that time he was living in the Valley, about 30 minutes away, and he owned a janitorial supply store. He agreed with my mother to see us on Sundays. He'd pick us up and we'd spend the day eating fast food, which was a real treat, since during the week we mostly ate only Korean. He'd take us to picnic at parks or on the beach. Occasionally, he took us to Disneyland or Magic Mountain.

During the rest of the week, we lived with my mother, who worked the graveyard shift at restaurants, until she eventually owned her own clothing store in a working-class neighborhood southeast of Los Angeles. Every day was hard for her which, at the time, seemed so incongruous with how my father lived. He never had to cook or clean for us or take us to school. He just got to do the "fun things" with us, and I resented him for that. I couldn't enjoy myself on our day trips, because I'd find myself thinking about my mother, and how she hadn't had time off in years, and how she ate the same food every day, and never slept because she worked so hard and then rose early in the mornings to get us ready for the day. Did my father want her to suffer? Was it because he felt so alone in his life, that he left her alone in hers?

¤

A few days after the cremation, my sister and I paid for a boat to take us out to spread his ashes. It was a beautiful sunny day. And this was something we did together, holding the least expensive urn we could find and then tilting the ash and pieces of bone into the water. The wind picked up, blowing him into our faces, and we laughed.

Because my sister had to go back to work in the Bay Area, it was up to me, with the help of my boyfriend at the time, to pack up my father's belongings before the end of the month.

He'd led a fairly meticulous life in his one-bedroom apartment — there were file folders labeled and filled with brochures from places we had gone during "happier times" (Disneyland, Magic Mountain, SeaWorld). Framed photographs of my sister and me. I even found a few VHS cassettes of porn inside the living room's coffee table cabinet, which I swiftly, without looking at the titles, chucked into the trash.

We didn't know what to do with the larger objects — in particular, the furniture our father had dragged out of our mother's house when he'd run away. In the end, we ran into a man down the hall, who was moving into another unit. He was probably in his 40s. He had tattoos along his arms and neck. We asked him if he wanted any of the furniture and he took it all — the dining room set, the bed, the coffee table. Jackpot. The man looked elated.

¤

In the past, I had imagined my father living for a very long time. I would visit him every once in a while in the hospital. I would look at him, dying, and confront him finally for leaving us, for hurting us, for abandoning my mother. I would break him, turn him into dust with my rage.

I had also imagined the alternative in which I would just sit by his bedside quietly, and he would look at me, and I would have great pity, even love for him, not as my father, but as a man, who had come to this country to reinvent himself, but failed. I had pictured watching him for hours, for days, sad for him, but also finally relieved that I would never have to visit or call him again.

In the end, I never had to make the choice about how I would honor my father or not in his last days. Perhaps his death — though tragic at the time — protected him from his own frailty, from the indignities that would have come with age. He'd managed it: he'd finally run away for good.

But from where and to what? Does hurt have a location? Does it float in the air, surrounding us? Does it circulate in the veins, in the blood? How many generations does it take for trauma to leave the body? And are those entrapments, that which we must endure together, what make us family?

Looking through my father's shelves, I'd discovered a brochure for a cemetery. I realized then that he had actually considered buying a plot. And I thought of my sister and I dumping him into the ocean, his ashes flying back into our eyes and mouths: What could we do about it now? Where could we visit him?

The boat's captain had given us a certificate indicating the exact location where we'd scattered his remains: but where else would we find him — his grief, his pain? Not north, not south, not east, not west, but in the center, inescapably, within. ❖

IMAGE: PATRICK JACKSON, *SQUEEZE*, 2016. PLASTICINE, POLYURETHANE, EPOXY. 34 x 26.5 x 7.5 INCHES. COURTESY THE ARIST AND GHEBALY GALLERY, LOS ANGELES. PHOTO: JEFF MCLANE

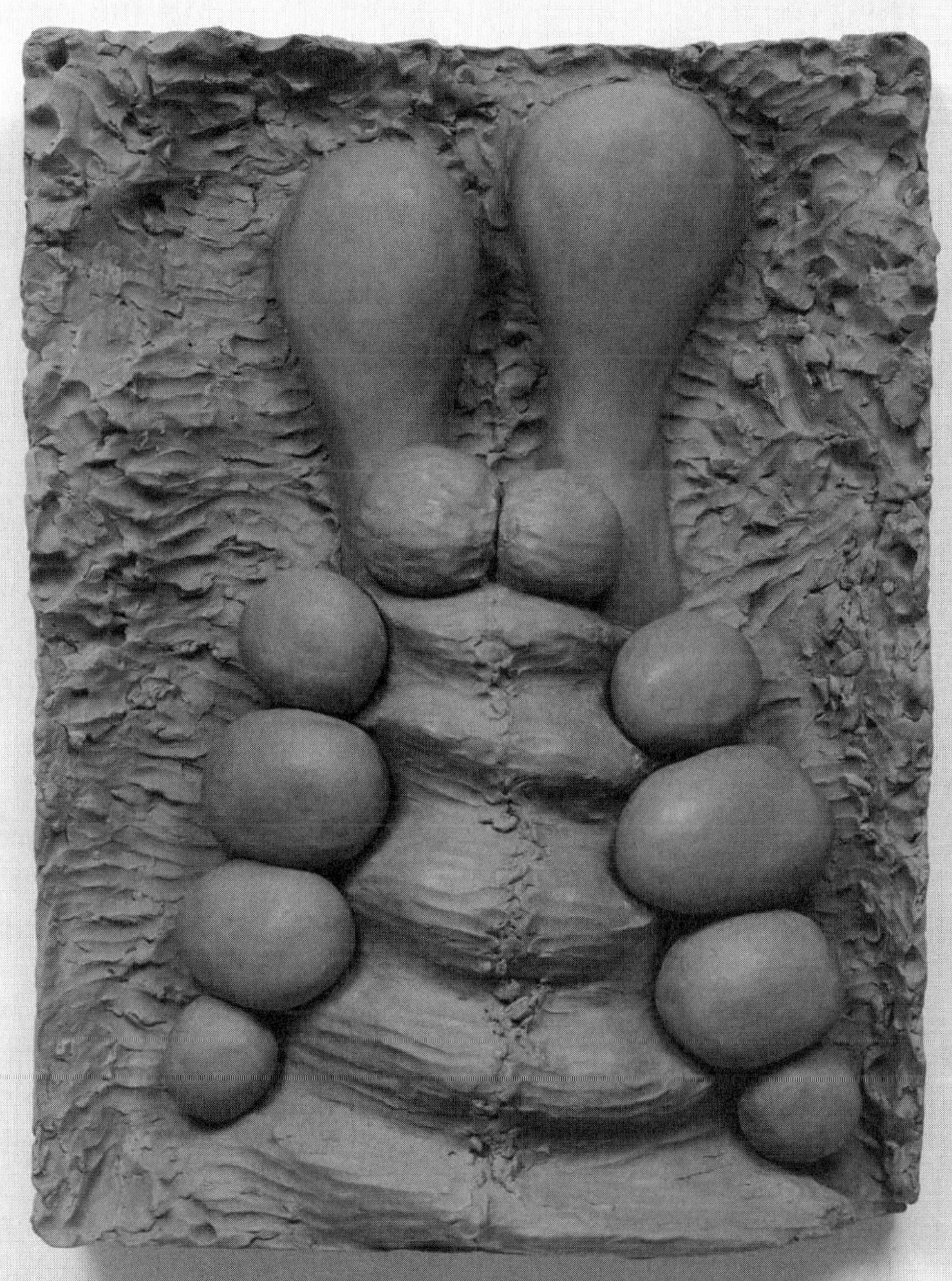

Recognition is the Misrecognition You Can Bear*

Ari Banias

Mostly a name feels like the crappy overhang I huddle under
while rain skims the front of me.

I admit it keeps me visible, the cool compromise
of efficient lighting, the agreement to call *this* that.

The coil of a compact fluorescent
I follow back to its root, inside a fixture
that imitates the moon

suitably enough, a For Rent sign hung in a window
where anyone might come to rest.

Alone on the avenues in open air I'm totally
outside myself, the coat but also
the thing inside the coat going around unseen,

unsure how I appear and whether
this constitutes a psychic problem
or simply the human condition.

Think of the interior of a lake,
almost entirely unavailable. Think of all
one face can transmit to another.

Mine looks far worse backward than I imagine
it does when you see it for me,
the two me's shining back
from the wildlife of your one.

Still, I refuse to miss when warmer light flattered us,
and the world burned out at alarming speed
while we brightened

at the sound of a bell, or hungered, pulling through
our respective mazes, not seeing them
for the variations on the same floor plan they were.

I still prefer the views from yours,
and to call the nowhere
most things come out of "The Blue."

Now I'm standing at the edge of this lake
Ohlone fished then white settlers turned
into a sewer. Settlers who fouled then moved

to clean it up as though to also own
the lake's rescue from ourselves
was a virtue. Volunteers in orange vests
sift out trash today with nets. My reflection

stares back from the refuse
crowded near its shore: a bobbing 5-Hour Energy,
two pair of jeans flattened
against lake's bottom, a sodden pillow

heavy with dreams I take uneasy
refuge in the facelessness of.

The empty water bottles and the dirty water
that are and aren't each other.

*The title is taken from Lauren Berlant's *Cruel Optimism* (2011).

Morphology

Ari Banias

I stood, a cloud of hair, teased up & sprayed in place, distinct
from the surrounding air. Somebody wore me on her head,

took orders. Withstood me

held and measured as a breath. Halo-gold, they said
I fixed her to the ground.

A fist and spoon they
kissed this into shape: say *me*, say *mine*, see /

as senator and its constituents.
My freedoms stirred until they turned constraints.

In mirrors, I eyed me; in storefront glass, in lakes. Touched tip of / to tip
to make a loop. This way, I felt both long and bunched. I felt like guts

some vultures who were me tore at.

I stood against a wall, under consideration, a paint chip taped there, half-unseen;

and leaning in prairie where wind combed & petted the tooth of me.

Some called I *she*, or *he* (or *it* or *they*).

Some taught me famous names, to drop the coins of these
in slots of conversation so with others I might feel like we.

But / at the shore of a sea, / on the pebbled, tar-smeared edge
of an island. There hungered or grumbled or stood an astonished /
I picked at like a splinter once part of something bigger.

These patches of dwindling snow, undifferentiated, but shapely.
Their yellow spots where something stood & peed.
And that admitting earth beneath.

CHERIE RACITI, *BLACK HOLE #2*, 2013. ACRYLIC AND FIBERGLASS, 17 x 16 INCHES FRAMED.

The Arab Baths

RICHIE HOFMANN

We removed our clothes and clung
to rough towels. There were decorative holes,
small and shapely planets
in a manageable cosmos,

through which artificial light rained down.
In the shower, touching oil to my hair,
I tried to imagine the lover as a mirror of the self,
but I was distracted by the tessellated wall of bats –

unlike us, each body cut
and polished to precisely the same shape
in a Moorish pattern that pleased me.
We moved between the baths

like men moving through the stages of life.
First, suspended like babies
in the warm water, in need of one another.
Then into heat, where candles flickered on a shelf

and mint tea filled a tiny flute of glass rimmed in silver.
Standing up, you were the glistening Tree,
until hot mist fell against my eyes,
obscuring everything.

When we plunged into the colder waters,
we could not feel the constituent parts
of our bodies anymore,
as if death were freedom from desire.

In the steam room, on a warm marble table,
I was preexistent, but then
the time-bound fragrances came: the air filled
with lavender, red amber, and flower of pomegranate.

The Prince: The Mind of Art

Richie Hofmann

If I were a love poet, I don't know to whom these various letters
would be addressed. Have you wanted
to inhabit the mind of art? To know, if for a moment
only, what was being made?

To know that you had made it – to know, in the precise instant
of its making, at least, what it was that you had made?

I thought the child
would change me, but he

was also, of course,
a fiction

to which
I felt, in the end, all too proximate.

All too proximate.
In the having

made him, at least –
do you understand?

Surely
you understand –

That's why we don't fall in love
with our children.

Bad Review

Abigail Thomas

Undear Editor,

You don't like these poems? You don't like these poems I write by myself and send to your magazine? You send these poems back to me with a little piece of paper that says you can't use these poems? You know what's going to happen to you now? A dog is going to go berserk and bite you in the leg. Your leg is going to get infected. A lot of bad things are going to start happening in your neighborhood. A crow is going to pick up a cigar butt and drop it down your chimney. Your house is going to burn up. Your wife is going to leave you for a potato farmer. Your magazine is going to fold. You know why? Because these poems you send back to me are good poems you're so dumb you jerk you don't even read these poems. Look, the little hair I pasted is still here! If I ever see you in the snow buried up to your neck I'm going to pull your hat down over your chin so people will think your head is just a piece of wool material. Nobody is going to help you. You are going to die in the snow with no magazine. Soon.

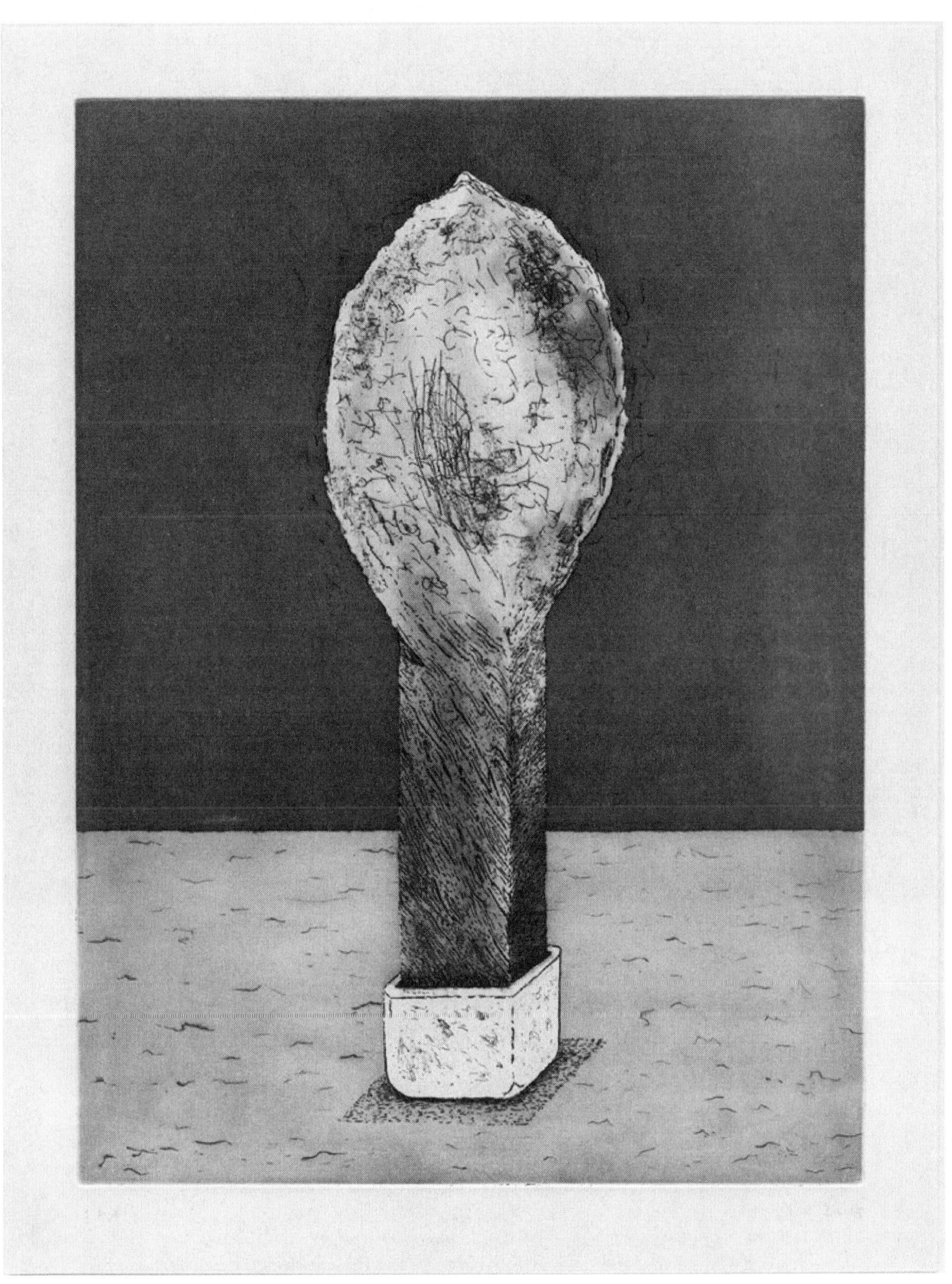

ZACHARY LEENER, *FIVE ETCHINGS (OBJECT)*, 2015, SOFTGROUND, DRYPOINT, SPITBITE, AQUATINT, 17 1/2 x 13 INCHES
EDITION OF 10 (3 AP), COURTESY THE ARTIST AND TIF SIGFRIDS GALLERY

THE PRIEST BLESSES JULIO'S WIDOW AND DAUGHTER AFTER THE MASS FOR HIS REBURIAL IN THE TECOMATLÁN CEMETERY. PHOTO: COLECTIVO EL ROSTRO DE JULIO

Exhumation

DIANA DEL ÁNGEL

TRANSLATED BY ROBIN MYERS

Then, all of the men of the earth
surrounded him; moved, the sad corpse looked at them;
he rose up slowly,
embraced the first man; started to walk ...

César Vallejo

ON SEPTEMBER 26, 2014, forty-three students from the Ayotzinapa Rural Teachers' College disappeared in the city of Iguala, Guerrero. Three others were executed: Julio César Ramírez Nava, Daniel Solís Gallardo, and Julio César Mondragón Fontes. The last of the three was tortured and murdered, his body dumped on a dirt road with the skin of his face stripped off. The photograph of his flayed face circulated online on Saturday, September 27, which is how his wife, Marisa Mendoza Cahuantzi, also a teacher, learned of her husband's death — she recognized his clothing.

Marisa and Julio had an infant daughter, just two months old at the time of Julio's execution. Marisa and her lawyer, Sayuri Herrera Román, undertook a legal process with the goal of exhuming Julio's body and performing a new autopsy, one that would be carried out by the Argentine Forensic Anthropology Team (known as EAAF, its acronym in Spanish). This procedure was necessary because the first autopsy, conducted by a forensic pathologist in Iguala, included no record of torture: the results insinuate that the flaying of Julio's face was caused by "local fauna."

The exhumation took place on November 4, 2015; due to bureaucratic delays and the general disinterest shown by relevant officials, the re-exhumation wasn't performed until February 12, 2016. On June 7 and 29, the two forensic teams (the EAAF and the team affiliated with the Department of the Attorney General) met with Julio's family to discuss the results of the second autopsy. Both teams agree that the cause of death was traumatic brain injury and that the 64 fractures found in his body constitute proof of torture; a year after his death, it was impossible to determine the cause of his facial injury. With the second autopsy now complete, the Department of the Attorney General will be asked to open a new line of investigation on torture as part of its previous inquiry, which is conducted at the federal level.

¤

DAY ONE, CHAMBER SIX: NOVEMBER 4, 2015

"WE'RE GOING TO GET STARTED," says the judge from Tenancingo, the official responsible for the exhumation of Julio César Mondragón Fontes.

Under the white tent provided by the Argentine forensic experts and pitched half an hour before, the diggers start shoveling into the past. We're here to uncover the truth of what happened on the night of September 26, 2014.

To do so, we've had to travel back and forth from Iguala, Tenancingo, and Toluca; we've pursued new appointments with government agencies; finally, we've reached today. The media, attracted by the morbid pull of the story, showed up early. Unfortunately, though, they haven't been interested in documenting all of the negligence and arbitrariness that has brought us here. They haven't paid much attention to the prosecutor Arely Gómez's failings either (she never released the date of the exhumation), or to President Enrique Peña Nieto's neglect — he was provided with a CD containing the photos taken by specialist Vicente Díaz Román, but these photos still haven't come into the possession of the attorney general's experts, because the corresponding letter was never sent at all.

On this day, Wednesday, November 4, the cemetery still wears the trappings of the Day of the Dead: spikenard, chrysanthemums, and Madonna lilies are everywhere. The sun bears down on us, and the tent is encircled by all manner of police: ministerial, state, and federal. First, the diggers remove the stone cross, laid just over a month ago to mark the anniversary of Mondragón's death. Then they remove the metal cross, placed by his widow and young daughter. We hear the shovel strike the earth for the first time — periodically interrupted by the judge's brassy voice ordering onlookers to refrain from taking photos, to stay behind the barrier, to do nothing. Within the first enclosure, formed by the police and a ring of caution tape, are the judge, her two court clerks, the lawyer, the widow, and the 22 specialists who will conduct the expert inspections for this second autopsy: seven are from the EAAF, seven belong to the Department of the Attorney General, and four were sent by the defense team for the police officers — with symmetrical irony, also 22 — charged with Julio's murder. Sanitation and fumigation staff are also present, as are other federal, state, and municipal officials.

Within a short time, beside the hollow that Mondragón's grave is becoming, a mound of soil swells until it reaches the height of the wall surrounding the cemetery. It seems impossible for so slight a space to hold so much earth. The first object uncovered is a small wooden box in the shape of a coffin. "There's the shadow," someone says, and proceeds to explain that the box contains what's left of the wax, fallen flower petals, and the quicklime that forms a cross for the vigils. Stored together and buried with the person himself, these elements are known as the shadow of the deceased. So the first thing to come out of the ground is Julio's shadow, which is swiftly measured and opened to ensure that the box contains nothing else.

A boot sinks the blade of the shovel into the dirt. With one shovelful after another, the metal finally hits the stone slab that covers the coffin. The diggers' labor intensifies; now they have to break stone. Chips of rock spray out from the center, and then, shard by shard, not only the slab but Mondragón's first burial breaks open — a burial undertaken amid enormous pain, and quickly, out of fear that the body would be stolen.

The physical exhaustion belongs to the diggers; the emotional exhaustion falls to the relatives who are now unearthing, in their own memories, the last days of September and the first of October, when Julio César Mondragón Fontes was interred. His mother busies herself in preparing and offering bread, chocolate, and lemonade to everyone in attendance. His wife Marisa has remained tirelessly attentive to the diggers' and specialists' every move. She appears calm — we try to accompany her however we can.

With great dexterity and several ropes, the diggers manage to pull out the coffin. It will have to be opened for the relevant authorities and the family to verify that it contains a body. The necessary measures are taken: everyone must wear a facemask; only family members may be present; all protocols must be obeyed. The coffin is blue with silver-plated decorations, but it has rusted a bit by now and the edges are still caked with dirt. The first task is to clean it, but not with water, which could seep inside and damage the evidence. Better to use toothbrushes and hand wipes.

After confirming that everything is in order, the diggers proceed to open the box. All we can hear is the creak of the top, one edge peeling away from the other like an eyelid, and Julio's body is exposed, looking out at us. The coffin's white cloth lining looks a little stained with rust and grime; Julio's bandaged head leans toward his right shoulder, beside the figure of the Child Jesus. The scapular on his chest is a path that leads us to his hands, still distinguishable, his fingers laced, holding some candles and a rosary; below, we can see his feet in their brown shoes, his favorites, a gift from his young wife. "He took good care of them," she recalls. The family members move past in small groups — aunts and uncles, cousins, nieces and nephews, in-laws, wife — and stand before Julio's body, facing him.

After a failed attempt at a procession toward Mexico City — everyone arrives as best they can; as for the police, thanks for nothing — we enter the Department of Expert Forensic Services and accompany the family in the final step of today's proceedings: that is, placing the coffin in the refrigerator, in the sixth chamber, with the requisite seals.

His body has been pulled up from where it was buried; we have brought back to life what they wanted forgotten; we have recovered evidence of what the Mexican government refuses to acknowledge: torture, a crime against humanity, perpetrated by the state.

Day Two: November 5, 2015

THE ATTORNEY General's Department of Expert Forensic Services is located where the Knorr Suiza condiment company once had its distribution center, along the Río Churubusco highway. The place couldn't be more uninviting: limited entry routes, a police-guarded access door, no signage, a vacant lot that functions as a parking area — the clatter of the suburban train eventually passing by. Across the street is another vacant lot; barely concealed by a crude enclosing wall, the spot is filled with dumped trash.

Mexico City's Forensic Medical Services (SEMEFO, its acronym in Spanish) has suspended all of its activities during the days of Julio's autopsy. The authorities, as requested by the Mondragón family, have set up a room for visitors to wait on site while experts work on his body. The scent of the room, no bigger than four by five meters, clarifies this building's purpose: after a few minutes, your sense of smell adjusts to it, or simply shuts down in response. The walls are lined with a kind of blue cloth. We hang up a poster displaying Julio's face, designed by Jan Nimmo, a Swedish artist; in front of it, we place some potted chrysanthemums and a flower arrangement that Marisa had received as a gift. Then others among us — we're all women here — lay out some fruit.

The first day of the autopsy includes a meeting for the experts working with the Argentine Forensic Anthropology Team (EAAF), the Department of the Attorney General, and the accused, respectively. The number of forensic experts has risen to 24. All the specialists have been here since 9:00 a.m., along with the public prosecutor from the Department of the Attorney General, the family's lawyer, and various members of the Interdisciplinary Group of Independent Experts (known as the GIEI); this group, established by the Inter-American

Commission on Human Rights as an alternative to the Mexican government-led investigation, studied the events that occurred in Iguala on September 26, 2014. Their results showed the duplicity of the official account.

Julio's family is in the adjacent room, talking a bit about the news articles published on yesterday's exhumation. After a while, Carlos Beristáin, a member of the GIEI, introduces himself and the coordinators of each expert team. To the family, he recites the list of agreements they've reached regarding how to carry out the tasks entailed by the autopsy. Among the most important decisions: The results will be released to the family first, before the press; in addition, the family will be consulted on every single procedure. The meeting, essential as it was, has gone on almost all morning; we decide that we'll break for lunch before returning to Forensic Services, so that Julio's body can be brought out before his family and taken to the examination room.

We find somewhere to eat in the wasteland surrounding the Forensics building. Almost the entire family has come from Tlaxcala and Tecomatlán — even Julio's grandfather is in Mexico City today — along with the psychologists who have been offering support, some friends, and other companions. Naturally, we don't speak about what's happening over lunch. We almost always chat about things going on around us, or, here, about the comical phrases decorating the restaurant: "Life is full of clothing sizes, so order whatever you want." When we head back to Forensic Services, we find the experts waiting for us before they open the sixth chamber, where Julio's body is stored.

Only Marisa and the family lawyer, Sayuri Herrera Román, can enter the chamber with the

Offering in memory of Julio César Mondragón in front of the Department of Expert Forensic Services during the second autopsy. Photo: Colectivo El Rostro de Julio.

experts. The rest of us, relatives and companions alike, watch through the Gesell camera as the coffin where Julio's body rests is reopened, and we see, as we'd seen the day before, the objects that accompany his remains: shoes, the figurine of the Child Jesus, the rosary. Each item is removed, measured, and meticulously examined before being packed away in a bag with the file number 212-2014, for Iguala, and 01-2015, for the Department of the Attorney General.

Bandages, still white, cover Julio's faceless face. It's impossible to look away from the image, painful as it is. Impossible, too, not to feel like something of ourselves stays inside the coffin when the experts close the lid. They wheel the casket into a room where the forensic analyses will be conducted. We return to where the family is waiting, directly above the examination area. It's Thursday, the day after Julio's body was pulled out of the ground.

By nightfall, the Argentine experts inform us that they've finished reviewing, cataloging, and packaging Julio's belongings. And so we go home, exhausted despite the fact that we've been sitting all day long as we wait.

Day Three: November 6, 2015

ON FRIDAY morning, Marisa, her parents, and the family lawyer have to meet with José Aarón Pérez Carro, the recently appointed director of the investigative office dedicated to the Ayotzinapa case at the Assistant Attorney General's Department of Human Rights. It isn't the best time to transfer Julio's case file from SEIDO (the Spanish-language acronym for the Assistant Attorney General's Office for Special Investigations on Organized Crime) to the new department taking it on: the bureaucratic limbo created by the lack of a single entity responsible for the case means, in this transitional phase, that the request for a DNA test could be stalled. After Pérez Carro promises to read the file — which is over a thousand pages long ("No problem!") — and evaluate the requests it contains, Marisa and her companions return to Forensic Services.

At some point between yesterday evening and this morning, I've noticed another room, adjacent to our small waiting area, with windows that look out onto a pile of boxes, all labeled Cocula Dump. In November 2014, the then-Attorney General of Mexico Jesús Murillo Karam gave a speech in which he declared that the students had been incinerated in the Cocula Dump and their ashes then thrown into the San Juan River. He called these conclusions, based on the official government investigation, the "historic truth." If I had any faith in the historic lies spread by the Department of the Attorney General, I'd think that the decision to accommodate us here — right next door to the supposed remains of Julio's classmates — was another form of torture.

I walk down the hall, looking for someone I can tell what I've just seen. I run into Sayuri, the family lawyer, with Dr. Retana, coordinator of Forensic Services. I approach them and find myself engaged in one of the strangest and most disheartening conversations I can remember. The doctor asks us to take down the blue poster printed with an image of Julio wearing a red t-shirt and hat (red was his favorite color); one of the phrases printed on the poster, in large white letters, reads, "Memory, justice, truth, and reparation for Julio César Mondragón Fontes. We haven't forgotten you, friend; we're still looking for justice." According to Retana, the poster could be offensive (he never tells us to whom), because a service worker, or someone along those lines, could see it and misinterpret the word "justice" (he never clarifies the possible meanings of this interpretive deviation), and so the director of the facility, upon hearing of the worker's misunderstanding, could reprimand Retana himself.

We ask in near-unison: In what sense is it offensive for a family to acknowledge their search for justice? How could a poster that has accompanied us in so many different events be offensive? Is the administration of this office really so inclusive that they would take a service worker's opinion so directly into account? Is any unknown person's perception more important than the suffering of the victims? When exactly did the word "justice" become inappropriate in our nation of impunity? In response to these questions, the doctor simply repeats what he told us at the beginning; the conversation goes nowhere. After a while, we tell him that if the director should reprimand him, we'll assume the consequences ourselves. "Don't worry," we say. In a final attempt to convince, he says — hardly surprising in a country that runs on simulations — that perhaps we could fold over the part of the poster where the offensive phrases are printed and show only his face. We refuse.

I keep thinking about how people are more afraid of words than of a face that no longer exists — a face whose very absence is the reason why we're all here.

After the incident with the coordinating doctor, we rest for a bit, chatting about mundane things, until two experts come upstairs — one from the EAAF and another from the Department of the Attorney General. The Argentine specialists tend to work in constant communication with the victims' family members; in Julio's case, making use of the fact that the relatives are located in the room directly above the examination area, they'd agreed to meet at the end of every workday to summarize the progress made and consult them on subsequent steps. It's a humane way to work. Astonishingly, the attorney general's experts have decided to do the same; at any rate, they try.

One of the crucial measures in examining Julio's remains involves separating his cranium from his spinal column; this is necessary in order to take X-rays from all possible angles. This information itself is hard to hear, but something about the way the expert conveys the information — he's with the Department of the Attorney General — makes it even harder; it suggests that something in Julio's body won't go back into the coffin with him when he's reburied. Marisa's face shows the anguish the news is causing her, and she looks around at all of us. But this is a decision that only she can make, so we just look back at her with as much love as we can. When Karla, the Argentine specialist, clarifies that nothing will be removed from Julio's body, and that they'll arrange some bones beside some other ones when they're finished so that he'll look the same as before, Marisa gives her consent: "Whatever has to be done," she says. "That's why we took him out."

Marisa has visibly changed since the last time I saw her in the Zócalo (main square) of Mexico City. She could barely give interviews then without weeping. I think of the photo taken of her just after she'd given birth to her daughter, her face still childlike; now her expression is that of an adult, a woman who grew up all at once.

Steve Symes is a bone expert, the best in the EAAF; in fact, the procedure was scheduled to suit his agenda. He doesn't speak Spanish, but he communicates deftly enough to transmit his enthusiasm for his work and his empathy for the victims. Beside him is another EAAF specialist who will serve as the translator. Steve explains he has found hairline fractures in at least 10 of Julio's front ribs (the human ribcage has 12 front and back ribs), and in order to take X-rays they'll need to dismantle the bones and remove their soft tissue — which means in turn that they'll be placed in hot water ("cook" is the verb Steve uses) until the ribs themselves are exposed. Afterward, the bones will be set back into place, but the body won't look the same as before; that is, it's possible that they won't be able to reclothe Julio, since only disjointed bones will be left. Marisa's expression slowly comes apart. The specialist says he understands the complexity of the decision and that he isn't expecting an immediate response; it can wait until tomorrow. Another option, he adds, is that he could cut only the part of the bone that's directly involved (to use the experts' term). The markings on some of the bones are minimal, he says, such that an uninformed person might not be able to detect them at all — but he can, and that's why he'll need to study them. Studying them could determine the force used in fracturing the bones and the direction the blows came from. We all sit in silence when he leaves.

Raymundo, from the Guerrero-based Colectivo Contra la Tortura y la Impunidad (Collective against Torture and Impunity), met Marisa when she went to the Ayotzinapa Rural Teachers' College before traveling to Chilpancingo, where she collected Julio's body in September 2014. As soon as he heard about the exhumation, he contacted her and asked to accompany her throughout the procedures; he knows how difficult they are. Respectfully and steadily, he asks if he can share his opinion; Marisa assents with her eyes. "What the experts are going to do is accelerate the process that would happen naturally — the soft tissue eventually disappears underground and only the bone is left before it turns to dust." When he puts it this way, it does sound like something natural; still, we know that none of what's happening here could possibly be so. "This is painful for us, but it can't hurt Julio anymore; Julio is resting now."

Marisa looks to her mother and father, who have been with her day after day. Her father seems to agree that the procedure should be carried out, but ultimately both parents say that they'll support her no matter what she decides. One of the therapists, who have accompanied Marisa and Julio's family throughout their mourning process, proposes that Marisa wait until tomorrow to discuss the situation with Julio's mother, brother, aunts, and uncles. This way the decision won't be hers alone. Marisa's expression relaxes a bit as she listens to this suggestion, and she agrees that it sounds like the best way forward. Without anything else to do for now, we leave the facility to prepare for tomorrow.

Day Four: Saturday, November 7

JULIO WAS LEFT ON the side of the road. Alone, surrounded by earth. Originally from Mexico State, he was the only student at the teachers' college who didn't live in Guerrero; he was living with Marisa in Mexico City by then. Although his murderers left us his body, they took away his face. They wanted to tear his smile from memory — which is why, on the action planned for today, November 7, we've decided to bring it back.

When we reach Forensic Services, Julio's family has already gathered together, deliberating about what Steve Symes had proposed the day before. The situation is intimate and delicate enough that we don't go into the room. A few hours later, we're informed that they have approved the full procedure required for X-raying the ribs; they also endorse the implementation of a genetics analysis. They won't consent to another exhumation after this one, so they want Julio's body to undergo all possible tests now. This investigation is marked by the absence of his face.

We've been waiting along the street adjacent to Forensic Services, under the bridge that supports the Circuito Interior freeway. People who have come to march give us votive candles and flowers; we wait for parcels of lime to arrive, along with some members of the SME (the Spanish-language acronym for the Mexican Union of Electricians) who are coming to set up the sound system. Guadalupe from CLAP (the Spanish-language acronym for the collective Conspiradores Libres del Aprendizaje, or Free Conspirators of Learning) shows up first; she managed to print a five-by-seven-meter poster this very morning, using a negative of Julio's face that his sister provided last night. Along with other colleagues, we start to prepare a small offering around the poster of Julio's face. Here, we'll welcome the group that has set out from the Plaza de las Tres Culturas, or Plaza of the Three Cultures — sorrowfully famous as the site of the student massacre on October 2, 1968 — and will march to Forensic Services in solidarity with Julio and his family while the final forensic inspections are carried out.

Around the poster's white cloth, where black lines trace the contours of Julio's smile, we set out the gladiolas and votive candles. Another colleague arrives with sawdust, half of it dyed black and the other still its natural color; this is what we'll use to fill in Julio's face. Others mix water and lime — makeshift paint we'll use on the wall facing Forensic Services. "Justice for Ayotzinapa" and "43" are some of the phrases written around the large-scale photos of Daniel Solís Gallardo and Julio César Ramírez Nava, both also executed on the night of September 26. Since the Day of the Dead was just days ago, we've found lots of leftover paper, lending a little color to the gray walls surrounding the facility. Our friends from the SME quickly set up the platform and sound system right in front of the bridge, so that people scheduled to speak later on won't suffer from the sun that's been blazing overhead since noon.

Julio's family leads the small march as it approaches. I'm told that Marisa has wept almost the whole way here and they're not sure if it's a good idea for her to speak with the microphone. Right behind the family are students from the Ayotzinapa teachers' college, all classmates of Julio's who have closely followed his case. It's easy to imagine Julio among them, laughing, walking. They're accompanied by other people who are here in solidarity; although it's a small march, it's a warm and moving demonstration. They arrive with posters painted for Julio, printed with stencil drawings of his face, and they've been painting walls along the way. Now, in front of Forensic Services, they take up their places and hold up posterboards spraypainted with Julio wearing his emblematic hat.

The Banda Costa Chileña, which plays *son* music from Guerrero, keeps us company as we put the final touches on the collective offering: the votive candles, flowers, and fruit that the marchers brought with them from the Plaza de las Tres Culturas. The sun is setting outside Forensic Services; when Mercedes, the director of the EAAF, returns to the facility after lunch, she is surprised to see everything we're doing to accompany her efforts. Entering the lab where the rest of the experts have been working all day, she tells them what's happening outside.

While some gradually fill in Julio's face on the poster on the ground with handfuls of sawdust, others, both family members and other companions, read excerpts of Julio's biography. They read in first person: what we want is to bring him back among us, to make him appear. Some of Julio's relatives read passages. When it's all over, we start to clean up; we leave the flowers and the candles behind, but we take Julio's face with us.

Around 9:00 p.m., we reenter Forensic Services: the specialists want to say goodbye to the family, since it's their last day here. We're joined this time by Eduardo Maganda, general secretary of the Ayotzinapa student committee. One of Julio's friends, "Chesman," offers up his own sweatshirt to accompany Julio in the coffin. We ask Eduardo to put it on so we can take a few photos; half-joking, all laughing, we ask him to model for us. Marisa has a notebook of messages for their daughter Melisa and starts passing it around so that we can each write a few words. It's hard to know what the right ones might be — what can we say to a little girl who's been born with such a legacy? But we all put something down. I don't remember what I wrote.

Steve Symes then comes upstairs, along with two of his students who have come to assist him in the forensic studies of Julio's body. His flight leaves the next day, and it's important for him to say goodbye in person. This is the first time in his entire career, he tells us, that he's worked directly below where the family of the body is waiting. He seems moved and excited to recall what Mercedes told him about the event we organized outside — even though they couldn't hear anything indoors, he thinks what we did was important; he thinks, in Julio's case, that what's happening in Mexico could make a difference. Marisa gives him one of the stencil prints made by our colleagues and asks someone else to write a phrase of thanks. Steve accepts the gift, touched, and rolls up the posterboard. I watch as he exits — he pauses to photograph the stenciling on the wall.

A Seed of Justice: Friday, February 12, 2016

Then shall thy light break forth as the morning,
and thine health shall spring forth speedily:
and thy righteousness shall go before thee;
the glory of the Lord shall be your rereward.
(Isaiah, 58:8)

After endless proceedings, Julio's reburial is scheduled for Friday, February 12. It's a complex day: the Pope's visit will turn the city upside down; fortunately, it will also attract the media. The appointment at the Department of Forensic Services is at 6:30 a.m. We all arrive bundled into jackets after a largely sleepless night. In addition to the family's companions, members of the GIEI are here in a show of support. Some of Julio's fellow students from Ayotzinapa have come, too; as soon as the sky lightens they pull out a large poster printed with the face of the young man who was once their classmate at the teachers' college. Also present are a member of the Colectivo Contra la Tortura y la Impunidad and Conrado Zepeda, a Jesuit priest who has suspended a seven-day silent retreat in order to be with us. Despite the early hour, the traffic is intense enough to delay Marisa, her family, and other companions. Between the bottlenecks and the usual bureaucratic requirements, it's past 7:00 by the time we enter Forensic Services.

Once again, we walk into a small room where Marisa's relatives, who have traveled from their hometown to join her, are waiting out the few minutes before the procedure begins. Little Melisa and her cousin, looked after by other people accompanying the family, will stay there until we leave for the cemetery. And here, today, as was also the case during the forensic analyses, the two forces fueling our struggle have met in this building: the concrete proof of the horrific past and the affirmation of life itself. This time, Marisa's sister and brother-in-law will help dress Julio's body. Once downstairs, near the sixth chamber, we pull on our face masks and those who will have direct contact with Julio's body put on special suits. Opening the refrigerator that has held its contents for over three months, the experts remove a white bag with Julio's remains inside. The laboratory smell should prepare us for what's next, but that's not how it happens.

When they open the white bag and Julio's body is exposed, I feel an enormous weight on my chest. As if the fetid scent of the lab had turned to lead, it presses in on the hole I feel in my stomach. I'm glad I haven't eaten breakfast. I wouldn't know how to guess the phase of decomposition in which Julio's body is currently found. But here we are — because Marisa decided to embark on this search for the truth, and those of us who have accompanied her along the way are trying to tell her with our very presence, today, in a moment as dark as this one, *you're not alone*. I think about how, aside from looking now, I'll have to write about this later: his torso is naked, his ribcage is sewn across the middle, his flesh ranges from light to dark brown in color, passing through purple; in place of a neck is merely a large swath of black skin, because his head had been removed; his limbs are simply stumps, because bones from his hands and feet were also taken out, and three pieces of tibia bone are missing from his left leg, newly cut for the DNA test. I know — as much as I repeat to myself that this isn't Julio; it's just an unfeeling composite of organic matter — that the image will hurt me for who knows how long; that the smell will etch itself deeply into all February mornings.

Together, an EAAF expert, another from the Department of the Attorney General, Marisa, her sister, and her brother-in-law start maneuvering to dress Julio's remains. First the dark gray pants: they lift one leg and then the other, both rigid. Marisa chose every garment. She and her family could have elected not to be there, as the forensic experts have reminded them at several points: "If you want we can do it ourselves, just the specialists." But she wanted to be here, and her family wanted to support her. In the end, only her sister and brother-and-law finish buttoning his lilac-colored shirt. Marisa tries to find a way to string a pendant around Julio's neck, a half-heart printed with her name. She manages to thread the chain through the first buttonholes of the shirt. Lovingly, Marisa places the red sweatshirt, folded twice and bearing the emblem of their school in Ayotzinapa, that Julio's friend gifted to accompany him in his rest.

Before they're done, they empty the contents of seven sealed plastic bags: bones from Julio's feet, hands, ribs, and skull. The Argentine specialist will perform this task. The procedure itself is simple: break the seals on each bag, show the contents to the camera supplied by the Department of the Attorney General (it has recorded the entire action), and then return the bones to their original place. Little by little, they place the different fragments, all X-rayed during the studies, where his neck used to be. Marisa has been only watching for a while now. At the end, we leave her alone with Julio and retreat to the other end of the laboratory. But the distance is too short for us not to hear her sobbing as she looks down at the remains of the body she so cherished: an upper jaw she loved, a lower jaw she kissed, a chest she adored, a forehead she longed for, teeth remembered for their smile.

When Marisa walks toward us again, I'm stunned to see that she's merely crying — I can't understand how tears are all we have in response to such unspeakable pain; I can't believe this is our only resource in expressing it. Ángela Buitrago, from the GIEI, helps her breathe as Carlos Beristáin takes her by the arm; slowly, she returns to us.

We leave the lab. Ángela helps Marisa step out of her special suit, and we get ready to leave for Tecomatlán. Staff from the Department of the Attorney General and the EAAF expert lift the new coffin, now carrying Julio's body, into the ambulance, accompanied by the old, and they put on the corresponding seals to safeguard the chain of custody. As the rest of us leave the Department of Forensic Services, Sayuri (the family lawyer) and the other participants in the bureaucratic process all review and sign the certificates and documents required for the case.

As with the exhumation, our caravan is a failure: the ambulance sets out far before the other cars are ready; the police vehicle drives over a bridge that's too small for the Ayotzinapa students' bus, and they have to detour almost all the way back to the beginning. When all is said and done, we reach the Tecomatlán cemetery at 1:30 in the afternoon, about two hours later than planned. The Tenancingo judge, who will bring these procedures to an end, is waiting for us. The mariachis hired by Marisa have reached the site, too. The judge renders an account of the steps being followed: breaking the seals, which appear both on the coffin and on the ambulance doors; verifying that the coffin contains the body; photographic records of the procedure provided by the experts from the Department of the Attorney General.

That morning, Julio's aunts and uncles and his brother, Lenin, had arranged for the town gravediggers to take care of his plot, so everything would go faster. People carry the coffin to a spot a few meters from where it will be buried. Father Conrado blesses the body we're about to plant. Then the judge officially confirms that it contains a corpse, and one of the experts from the Department of the Attorney General takes out the bags of belongings that have accompanied Julio since his first funeral: a book, a rosary, a figurine of the Child Jesus, a pair of shoes. All are returned to the coffin. When everything has been verified, they lower the lid. The judge's voice announces each action carried out by the specialists. As in Forensic Services, the attorney general and the court cameras have filmed every procedure in the cemetery. The wind carries the faint smell of death all the way to the police barrier. Some supporters from Pedregales ask if they are allowed to pray. "Just in your heads; no interrupting the protocol," the judge responds. After a ludicrous argument between the judge, health officials, specialists, and family members, it's decided that the old coffin will be buried in the same place, once the stone has been laid over the new one. Duly authorized, the mariachis play the song "Caminos de Guanajuato."

Julio's classmates wait along one side of the cemetery, extending the poster printed with his face. The rest of us gather around the police barrier or by the perimeter wall. The banner held up by an old woman reads, "Julio César, your face and your conscience shines in every one of us." Julio's aunts, uncles, and brother help the diggers fill in the gravel; one shovelful at a time, the hole is covered after its three months of emptiness. Many weep. When they're almost done, they lay in the small coffin, the one with Julio's shadow inside, and cover it with the remaining earth. After several more interventions, the judge finally announces that she's leaving; even before she crosses the threshold of the cemetery, we can hear the shouts of "Julio lives," "Julio didn't die, Peña killed him," and "Marisa, listen, we're with you in your struggle." We start placing red roses around the grave, and we lay a crown and white floral arrangements on top if it.

Conrado begins to officiate. His white robe is draped with a purple stole, made by the Comandanta Ramona — a Tzotzil indigenous leader in the EZLN, or Zapatista Army of National Liberation, who died in 2006. Providentially, the suggested passage for the first Friday of Lent is from the Book of Isaiah, 58:1-8, which says: "Cry aloud, spare not; lift up your voice like a trumpet; tell My people their transgression, and the house of Jacob their sins." The word of the Lord, says the priest. The tone of the mass is one of consolation, offering strength and solace in the continued search for justice. It's brief, but it leaves us with a sense of longing to work for a better world. ❖

Uncle, Eat

Vanessa Hua

SOMETIME AFTER LUNCH, Old Wu realized he'd been kidnapped.

On the way from the airport, his cousin had taken a detour. If he'd driven in circles, or gone the wrong direction, Old Wu wouldn't have known the difference. In the countryside west of Hong Kong on the Pearl River Delta, the rutted roads looked alike and the flash of return, of welcome, hadn't yet arrived. More than a half century ago, he left the hills green with pine and bamboo for San Francisco, and hadn't returned since.

His cousin wasn't the son of an aunt or an uncle, but a relative of some kind from the village, who possessed a wreck of a car, and had volunteered to fetch Old Wu. The cousin was a former construction worker whose time perched on skyscrapers had inflated his self-importance. Less than an hour into the drive, his cousin parked in front of a concrete building, a restaurant famous for the local specialty: *gay long*, rice flour dumplings pleated into the shape of ingots and deep fried. The air was muggy, swollen as a bruise. They were the only customers at the only table, and the only staff was his cousin's daughter, Little Treasure. She brought out platter after platter, refilled pots of jasmine tea, and a bottle of rice wine that Old Wu declined. She hovered, simpering and smiling like a courtesan.

Startling to find himself in high demand after his years among the bachelors of Chinatown. When Chinese first left for America to tunnel through mountains for the railroads and snatch gold from rivers, most were men. Though few fortune-seekers intended to settle, laws also barred most Chinese women, to prevent families from taking root.

During World War II, not long before Old Wu's parents sent him to America, the laws changed. Finding a wife had remained a competitive endeavor, and Old Wu hadn't much to differentiate himself as a suitor, just another waiter-turned-cook. Others had gone on to run restaurants, laundries, farms, and factories and move to the suburbs, but Old Wu never left. By the time families crammed into Chinatown's tenements, it was too late to start his own. The ancients had decreed a man should not marry after 30 years of age, and should not have children after 50, because the proper time for those things had passed.

Then his mother had written, insisting Old Wu marry. She was 93, he was 76. Come back, she told him. Come back and find a wife.

Little Treasure dropped off toothpicks and a bowl of lychees, and poured another cup of tea, but he refrained from drinking. He had a long ride ahead to the village, his leaky bladder didn't need more pressure, and the strong brew made him jittery. A few minutes ago, his cousin had excused himself to urinate and Old Wu should too. He didn't want to run to the latrines in the first moments of his homecoming, but when he tried to turn the handle of the restaurant's front door, it didn't budge. It must be stuck, the wooden frame warped and swollen. "Hey, hey," he shouted.

Little Treasure tugged on his elbow. "Uncle, eat." She looked at him coyly from beneath her lashes. "Does it taste like how you remember?"

"We filled ours with air." During his childhood, his family ate meat only once a year, during the Spring Festival, but this young girl had never known such want, only China on the rise and none of its turmoil. Turmoil that he had largely escaped by moving to America: the stunted crops and starvation of the Great Leap Forward, the book burnings and beatings of the Cultural Revolution, decades of strife and deprivation that his parents had spared him.

He knocked again and leaned his weight against the door. Locked. He searched for another exit, but didn't see another door, and the sole window was too small to squeeze through. He'd heard of brides abducted by grooms, but never a kidnapped groom! His cousin must want to present his daughter to Old Wu, to make her the first and most memorable candidate for marriage and the green card that came along with the deal. In time, she could sponsor her parents, her siblings, their spouses, and their children to immigrate. A prize her father wouldn't let slip out of his fingers.

"Uncle, eat." Little Treasure had a broad, plain face, placid as a cow, her beauty residing in the cascade of inky black hair that fell to her waist. In a tight t-shirt and flared jeans, she was as tall as him, and twice as strong, with the muscular arms of a model revolutionary. She could level weeds and enemies alike. She could pin him to the narrow bed that he now noticed beneath a calendar of beer models. "Uncle, he'll be back soon. Sit, sit. You've had a long flight."

He settled into his chair. Even if he escaped, he didn't know where he was or how far he'd have to walk to his village. Soon enough, his cousin would understand that love at first sight hadn't transpired. Little Treasure would have to wait her turn to be ranked and compared to the other women whom the village elders had selected for his consideration.

He ate another dumpling, the crust crispy yet chewy, filled with sausage, peanuts, chives, and water chestnuts. Little Treasure dug her fingers into his shoulders. Every bit of him clenched, his jaw, his gut, his toes.

"Uncle, let me." She kneaded the knots in his neck. She might be one of those girls who sold themselves in the cities. On occasion, he had visited those languorous, heavy-lidded women who charged by the hour, by the procedure, in the red-lit massage parlors a few blocks from Chinatown. He hadn't visited in years, not with the dried shrimp between his legs that hardly had the strength to take a piss.

Her hand crept to his thigh and he pushed it away. "Let me help you," she whispered. Her face burned.

He'd been mistaken. She wasn't a professional. He shuffled away, wondering if his cousin was spying through a crack, trying to catch Old Wu in an indelicate position. And who could blame him? China was becoming a superpower that launched astronauts into space, put on an Olympics breathtaking in its scale and magnificence, and might soon become the Middle Kingdom around which the world revolved. But for now, his cousin and Little Treasure remained mired in this backwater where Old Wu presented the best and only prospects.

Little Treasure wept, burying her face into her hands.

"Young maiden," he began.

"Young?" Her cheeks glittered with tears. "You should see who they have picked out for

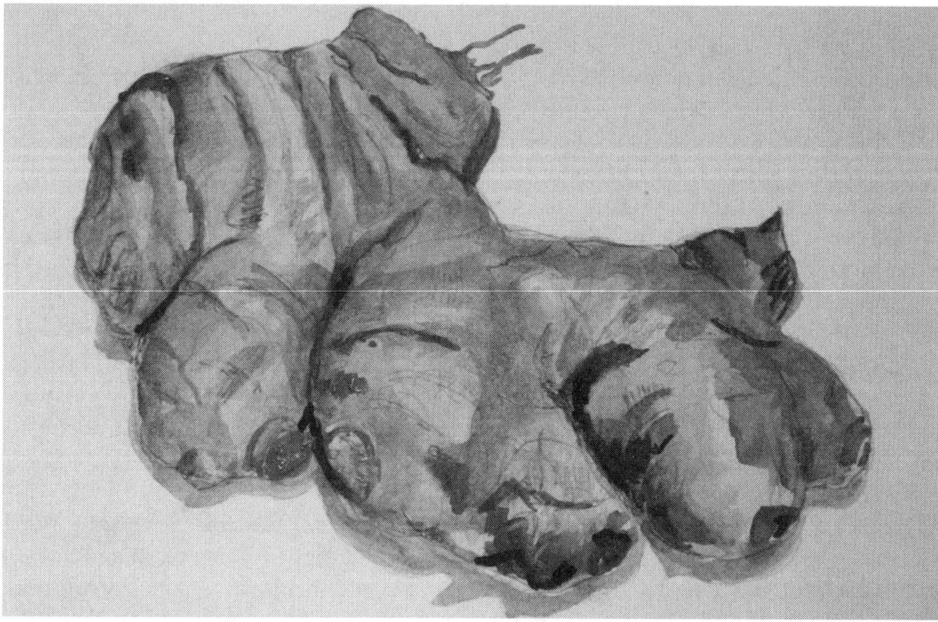

GINGER ROOT BY RAKKA

you, girls pried from their dolls. I'm a leftover woman."

Old Wu guessed that she was approaching 30 and still single. She told him after she returned from working in the city as a waitress she'd had a few marriage proposals, but her father held out, convinced she could make a better match.

"You don't want an old ginger root like me," Old Wu said.

"The older the ginger, the hotter the spice."

"When is he coming back?"

"As long as it takes." She sniffled and wiped her nose with the back of her hand. "You're my last chance."

"You're not old enough to be thinking about the end."

"No one wants meat that's gone off." Her bluntness surprised him.

"Call your father."

She pushed the bowl of lychees toward him, which he ate to cleanse his greasy mouth. He spit the shiny pit into his cupped palm, and he had another, savoring the sweetness. His mother used to peel lychees for him, digging in her thumbnail to break the flesh. Long ago, the emperor's concubine had pined for the taste in winter. With lychees crammed into saddlebags, imperial soldiers galloped north, handing off the precious cargo to the next rider each time the horse tired, completing the journey of two weeks in two days.

Old Wu had been his mother's firstborn and her favorite, the heap of rice in his bowl second only to his father's. The most tender greens, and the plumpest dumpling always piled before him. When he was very young, he followed her to the river, where she beat laundry against the rocks. How mighty she'd seemed! Warm mud squishing between his toes, sunshine heavy on his cheek, and the smell of the river, of wind on water and churned earth.

Little Treasure cleared the table, and he smelled the dank musk of her, straw and loamy soil and all at once he remembered his boyhood, the life he'd left behind and he was overcome with longing for this lost world. He closed his eyes, inhaling.

She tugged at the zipper of his pants, and he pushed her away, harder than he intended. She stumbled, crying out, and his cousin burst in, ready to catch Old Wu deflowering her. Old Wu pushed past him and found the car unlocked, the radio playing and keys in the ignition. He buckled himself into the passenger seat. He'd never learned how to drive.

His cousin told him to go back inside, with a smile that slid into a snarl. "We're not finished."

"We're late," Old Wu said. "You don't want to keep Ma waiting."

Ma, the final arbiter of any marriage. His cousin called for Little Treasure, who climbed into the backseat and they drove in silence for an hour in the land of the red earth laced with rivers, passing between centuries from one bend in the road to another. Farmers in straw hats and rubber boots tilled the fields with wooden plows and oxen, and at the next curve, squat factories interrupted. The pitted road was so narrow they had to drive into the oncoming lane to pass men pedaling carts loaded with sugarcane or sheet metal, before turning onto a dirt track that led to an arched gate marking the village entrance.

Money from relatives abroad and teenagers working in the cities, in factories and construction sites, as maids, security guards, and waitresses, had transformed the village. Crumbling mud bricks made way for concrete homes, a new schoolhouse, and a fish pond beneath a willow tree in the central plaza. But the village still lacked electricity, still lacked running water, still lacked opportunity.

Strangers, all. No one he remembered.

In his mother's house, Old Wu discovered a photo in a dusty plastic frame in the family's shrine, beside a pot of incense and a bunch of lychees. In the overexposed snapshot, tinged in orange and brown, he appeared miraculously young. His hair bushy as a fox's tail and his back straight as an iron rod, a man who should have had his pick of a wife. Shocking, to discover a piece of him had been here all along, in a village which had become abstract in his memories. He didn't remember who had snapped his photo in Chinatown, sometime in the 1970s, nor did he remember sending it to his mother, slipped into the translucent sheets of airmail, in which he never could reveal much of himself. She never learned to read or write, and her brief, sporadic replies came under a different stranger's handwriting each time.

For decades, she'd been a widow. If his mother expected him in his prime, she — and all the prospective brides-to-be — would be grievously disappointed. Only the brightness of his eyes remained, and a full set of teeth, of which he was exceedingly proud. If he'd stayed in the village, he might have become stooped, his hands shaky and his breath labored. He might have died. He was hardiest of the three siblings in his family and the sole survivor. He didn't remember Ma's face, only how she squeezed him so tightly he couldn't breathe the day he left the village. He'd been 10 years old.

From the deck, he watched his father, standing still as a pillar on the waterfront, until the ship slipped out of sight. His parents had borrowed to pay for his passage in San Francisco, resting their hopes upon his wiry frame. He entered under a false identity, becoming a Kwan, the alleged son of an American citizen. A name he repeated over and over to himself, a name that never felt right, that he never wanted to pass onto a wife or children. A name that prevented him from sponsoring visas for his true mother and father because in the eyes of the

US government, his parents-on-paper had already immigrated.

If he never saw Ma again, she could remain as vital and strong in his memories. Any minute, she would shuffle in here, her arms wide in greeting. She slept in here, beside the kitchen. She must be preparing his bed in the second room he'd paid for but had never seen. He'd bow to her, and present her the supplements she'd requested to help lower her blood pressure. "Ma?" he asked. She didn't answer.

His cousin eased Old Wu into a chair, telling him that she'd died a week ago in her sleep. A heart attack, the doctor declared, and there had been no way to get a message to him before he arrived.

Ma — dead? In San Francisco, she rarely crossed his mind. Now he reeled, as much as if he'd witnessed a car plowing her down. Because Old Wu didn't have a phone or an email address, it had been decided he should be told after his arrival. Who decided — his cousin? His cousin, who'd dined with him, offered a cigarette, pimped his daughter, but said nothing this afternoon. Old Wu wanted to flip the table and shove him to the ground. Watch his cousin's ugly face twist in panic, in fear, a fraction of what roiled in Old Wu.

No expense had been spared, his cousin was saying, and he scrolled through photos on his mobile phone, displaying wreathes and banners, and top-quality, slow-burning incense and the loudest firecrackers. "Three layers of silk garments and a pearl in her hand," he said. To light her way into the next world.

Ma was here. She was everywhere in this house, in the musty herbs she boiled for medicine, in the mud-spattered rubber shoes by the front door, as if she'd stepped inside a moment ago.

"Why didn't you tell me?" Old Wu's hands curled into fists.

"You'd had such a long trip," his cousin said. "You needed something to eat first. Bad news on an empty stomach, it's too much of a shock."

"You don't know what I need!"

"Don't I?"

Out by the car, Little Treasure was unloading Old Wu's luggage, heavy with gifts. Children swarmed around her. Old Wu staggered to his feet, knocking over the chair. Without Ma, he had no connection to this village. To China, his homeland alien as the moon. Dizzy, he hung his head, trying to get his bearings. His cousin tied something around Old Wu's arm — a strip of black cloth, to be worn for 49 days of mourning. Unfilial son. If only — if only he'd booked an earlier ticket, if only he'd come back last year, or five years ago. "Take me there."

His cousin ushered him down the crooked path to the cemetery and to the burial mound, heaped with wilting flowers and the ashes of incense and hell money, burnt offerings so she could enjoy the wealth she never had in life. The smells coated his tongue like a vile pudding. His brother and sister had passed away years ago, and their children hadn't attended the funeral. They had grandchildren of their own, and lived in distant cities after Old Wu's remittances had afforded them opportunities to leave. His father's grave was beside her, the grass clipped short and the stone marker wiped clean of mud. Other mounds were unkempt, overgrown with weeds, abandoned by forgetful, ungrateful descendants like Old Wu.

More villagers were coming up the path now, curious to meet their long lost cousin who lived in America. The crowd parted for a man whose body coiled with the power of a withheld punch, the headman who must have conspired to bring Old Wu here. A few young women — teenagers — had brushed on lip gloss, rouged their cheeks, and tied off their braids with satin bows. After he paid his respects to his mother, they probably would parade before him, like contestants in the Miss Chinatown pageant.

Did Ma have any say in the candidates? Were they kind to her, these potential daughters-in-law, to the poor granny who lived alone? He knew little of his mother's daily life. She must have relied on neighbors to fetch straw to light the stove, to boil water for her bath, and to weed the toughest patches. He couldn't have failed her more, no different from if he'd forced her to live in a pigsty. He couldn't stay here for a week. He couldn't bear to stay here overnight.

"Big Brother," his cousin said. Old Wu bristled. "You'll never have to worry sweeping her tomb. We're family, and we take care of each other."

Family? He had little in common with his cousin other than the vaunted ancestor from 10 generations ago, who'd settled and spawned in this damp patch of valley.

"I can't," Old Wu said. "I can't stay."

"But you've just arrived!" His cousin put an arm around Old Wu's shoulders, and lowered his voice. "The conditions at revered Granny's aren't up to your standards, but you can stay with me. I have a generator. A television. You'll have my bed. I'll sleep on the ground, Big Brother."

Old Wu jerked away. The air was hazy and overcast, and the heat so intense, he felt like an ant beneath a magnifying glass. "Cousin, take me to the airport."

"I promised revered Granny that I'd look after you." His cousin wore muddy loafers, with no socks, never able to escape his peasant habits, his peasant stink despite his boxy suit with the sales-tag dangling from the sleeve — purchased for the funeral? — and his sickening cologne.

"I'll make a ghost out of you!" Old Wu said. His cousin backed off.

"Stay." Little Treasure clutched an empty sack of the foil-wrapped premium chocolates he'd purchased at a Chinatown drug store. She must have opened his suitcase, dug through his belongings and distributed his gifts to the children, whose mouths were streaked brown. She must have tossed aside his yellowing undershirts and underpants stippled with holes, in front of dozens of onlookers. He wanted to clap his hands over his crotch.

"A good daughter," his cousin said. "She massaged revered Granny's legs every day, and read her stories from newspapers." He lowered his voice. "It was Granny's last wish. For you to marry. To marry Little Treasure."

This entire trip might have grown out of this man's plotting. Old Wu's mother could have been ailing for a while. If his cousin had feared the end of the remittances, he might have written the letter ordering Old Wu to come home and marry. He couldn't trust this man with sly eyes and oily lips, couldn't trust anyone here not to tear the clothes off his back and the shoes off his feet.

The neighboring village wasn't far, a cluster of homes on the other side of the patchwork of tilled plots, and from there, he'd find a ride to the airport. He'd sleep in the departures hall if necessary until he could get a flight to San Francisco.

He lurched away from his cousin and Little Treasure, and into a pack of children who clapped and spun and hugged him, all the descendants he'd never had and never would. The faces offered glimpses of Old Wu's lost siblings, his lost father and lost mother. Their common blood, their vitality that he might draw upon, as if from a well.

Though their welcome was a show, a shakedown, though he knew the children flocked to him out of survival and not out of love, he would never be received like an emperor again. For most of his life, he lived a lowly existence. For tonight, he deserved VIP treatment. Tomorrow he'd walk out of the trap they laid. Their warm, grubby hands reached for his, and he followed.

¤

The crescent moon hung heavy and low in the sky, ripe enough to pluck on a warm night, of the sort that San Francisco never had, that kept people up and outdoors, that he hadn't realized he missed. Every table, chair, bowl, and plate in the village had been carried into the plaza and set for a feast grand as a wedding — grander. The villagers greeted him with claps and cheers, and he fought the urge to duck his head, feeling unexpectedly embarrassed.

He wanted to impress them. Not for his sake, but for Ma and her legacy. The headman served him first, the most tender fish, succulent beef, and broccoli green as jade. Everyone watched, perhaps worried that he might have returned with tastes too refined for the likes of their country cuisine. When he swallowed and took another bite, relief swept over their faces. Old Wu was still like them, despite the years and the distance between them.

The headman poured the first of many cups of rice wine. Old Wu spat silvery pin-bones into his bowl. With a chopstick in each hand, the headman raised the fish aloft and Old Wu picked off the filet underneath. The taste was sweet and faintly muddy as the pond where it had been raised. If you were Chinese, flipping a fish was bad luck — akin to capsizing a boat — no matter where you lived, no matter how long ago you left the village.

The lion dancers cavorted in threadbare, ill-fitting costumes, followed by a brass band with braying, out-of-tune trumpets and arrhythmic drums, and a children's chorus that sang a tune about a wise old man of the forest. Afterward, the performers marched by. He clapped until his hands throbbed, but the soloist's eyes glittered with tears, a girl no more than eight. She trembled and he wondered if her parents had threatened to beat her, to deny her food if she failed to stir the heart of Old Wu.

Little Treasure caught his eye and raised her hands, hinting he should stand. Only when he jumped to his feet did the soloist straighten. To his surprise, everyone else rose too, imitating him. He wasn't used to people watching him so closely and the attention unnerved him. He smoothed his hands down his shirt and over his rumpled hair. All his life, he'd worked in the background, in the kitchen, the customers focused on the dish before them and never the man who chopped, sauced, steamed, and stir-fried — even if his hands at the gas stove were fluid as a calligrapher's.

If he hopped on one leg, clapped his arms over his head, would they copy him? He took his seat. The breeze rattled the bare branches of the sycamore trees and carried the scent of burning straw from the stoves of the communal kitchen, where grannies emerged with the next course. A crone set a platter before him and pinched his cheek. "Little Wu!"

He pulled away. "You don't remember me?" she asked.

He wanted to be generous, as the others must have been to his mother and other abandoned grannies in the village. He squinted at her. "I might."

"My brother shared a desk with you at school. We all played together."

Played together? She seemed ancient as Ma. "That songbird, that's my granddaughter. Some say she looks just like me, when I was her age."

"Very talented." Old Wu reached for his chopsticks.

"She'd earn her keep."

His chopsticks hovered over his bowl.

"She could help with chores, washing and cleaning and cooking. And she could bring in money singing, too. If you adopt," she whispered. It seemed she didn't want anyone else to hear her scheme.

"Little Wu." Her gaze frank, and her smile suggestive, missing most of her teeth, leaving brown nubs. She leaned in again, her voice throaty and her scent musty. She placed her hand on his forearm. "Remember those afternoons in the apple orchard?"

The headman took her by the arm and all but shoved her toward the kitchen. Apparently, Old Wu had passed into legend. Everyone had stories about him, even those born decades after he'd left, stories that he himself didn't remember. Like the time he'd gotten lost and the village had fanned out with lanterns at sundown, calling his name. He'd been a handsome toddler, with a head round and hard as an iron bowl. Never still, headlong toward the horizon. His mother had feared he'd been carried off, sold to a childless couple who wanted a son, or captured by bandits who ate the flesh of the young to give them the strength of 10 men. A miracle, when the headman found him asleep, curled in a haystack. Later, he fell ill with a high fever, and might have died but for his mother, who begged a market customer for help, a doctor's wife, and procured a vial of an expensive medicine new to the country — penicillin. He could have, should have died a hundred times before he turned 10. In his mother's telling, he'd been fated to leave the village, and fated to remain abroad, the only way she could accept his long absence.

Dark blots whizzed across the sky, flapping their wings. Bats. He hadn't seen one in decades, not in Chinatown. To Ma, bats symbolized prosperity and good luck, and she had embroidered a flock onto the hem of the shirt, those knots and nubs he rubbed in the dark on his voyage to America. All at once, he remembered that she was gone.

He hung his head until dancers jostled before him, dropping any pretense of cooperation and coordination. Many of these teenagers might be candidates, faced with a choice of marrying him or leaving for the cities to find work. He knocked over his empty cup. Tipsy after too much rice wine, he tilted the cup toward the dancers, toasting their efforts, and a handful giggled.

They tried to jump higher than each other, as if the strength in their calves and the spring in their thighs might nudge them ahead in the competition. The scratchy strings ended on the cassette tape, and the dancers skipped off. Throwing backward glances at Old Wu, a few crashed into each other like bowling pins.

He burped. His stomach swollen on his skinny frame, like a snake who has swallowed a chicken whole. He drummed his fingers on his belly, his shirt untucked, pants unzipped. He had no intention of taking a wife whose youth would only age him. He knew that now.

At the children's table, Little Treasure passed out steamed buns. She filled their bowls and wiped their faces with brisk yet loving ease. A maiden aunt who must long for her own brood. She noticed him watching and smiled.

After a night of performing for him, didn't the villagers deserve a show of their own? He tossed up a spongy bun and caught it with a flick of his hand, and added two more. He pushed through his intoxication, his hands remembering how to keep the buns in the air. Two up, one down. One on one on one. Something he'd picked up along the way, in his years alone. Juggling, another marvel from the village benefactor, and this time, when everyone clapped, he'd earned their applause.

Little Treasure brought him a cup of tea. His mouth puckered from the brew, which had been steeped for too long, but he swallowed.

¤

Before going to sleep, he barricaded the front door with the kitchen table and two chairs. He didn't want to wake up to the midnight gropes of Little Treasure, or any of the wretched young beauties. He collapsed onto his mother's narrow bed, trying to find a comfortable position, too tired to change into his pajamas. His cheeks numb from the wine, and his belly bloated as carrion. Soon someone scratched at the front door. "Uncle."

"Go away," Old Wu said. "It's late." Little Treasure's breathing was labored, and he pictured her slumped on the ground, pressed against the door.

"It's awful," she said. "You didn't get to say goodbye."

The first and only time that anyone had acknowledged his loss. His pulse was racing now, and he thought he might vomit. He tore off his sweater.

"Granny told me you never stopped sending money, not like most everyone else who leaves and forgets," she said.

Some months more, some months less, enough to build a house for his parents that didn't dissolve in the rain, to pay for medicine, the school fees of his niece and nephew, and a dignified funeral for his father. And for his mother, too.

"Uncle, I have something you want."

"Go to sleep, Little Treasure."

She laughed a madwoman's laugh. "Let's go for a dip. The moon — it's bright as day."

She'd drown in the pond, her body bloated and her hair floating like weeds. He pushed aside the table and chairs, sweating from his exertions, his pulse frantic as oil on a hot wok. He opened the door.

Little Treasure set down an insulated bottle on the kitchen table. She sat him on his mother's lumpy bed, put a cool hand against his forehead and he leaned against her until his breathing steadied. She reeked of liquor, of regret, sour and sharp.

"Too much," she murmured to herself. Too much food, too much drink at the feast?

She poured tea into two cups from her bottle. Hot and bitter, but he was thirsty.

"Granny said you had your own place, and that you ate all your meals in restaurants," she said. He nodded, but couldn't find the words to explain that by American standards, he was poor, and that the more you earned, the more you wanted.

"And that you had a mansion. Like this." She picked up a rumpled magazine that fell open to a picture of a grand estate with the white columns and ornate trim of the White House. What he'd achieved in America hadn't been enough for his mother, not compared to the other stories of riches from Gold Mountain. She had to invent the son she wanted, the son she deserved, and these lies explained the desperate interest on these families marrying off their daughters. Enough wealth to support a wife, to support them all.

"A new car, every other year." She scooted beside Old Wu, her thigh pressing against his. She poured him another cup of the bitter brew. "I like the BMW X5, or the Audi A4."

"I prefer Ferrari." He couldn't stop the lies from tumbling out, the lies that would raise his mother higher in the village's esteem. Little Treasure touched his chest and heat stirred in him.

Who didn't want a rich American uncle, who filled you with a sense of possibility, of prosperity close enough to touch? In your dreams, you escaped the prison of your circumstances and danced on the streets paved with gold. Little Treasure put her hand on his, her fingers stroking, circling until he felt pooled in sunshine. She'd left her tea untouched. Tainted, sprinkled with powdered rhino horn or another sexual tonic to raise him from the dead? Her lips brushed against his, and he fell into her. ❖

Good Questions

Rachel Eliza Griffiths

Who did you bleed for?
                    The body required primary color. Iron. Jewels.
Did you answer the void?
                    Yes, sometimes.
What did you give back after you gave everything up?
                    Isn't that the same?
Answer your answers.
                    Where is she? What has been done?
What are you trying to articulate?
                    There were birds singing the very next morning. Why?
When did the arrangements begin?
                    At her birth. When my birth began –
                                        At the red stones.
Did you already know?
                    Birth & knowing had been established at once, you see.
You prayed before or after?
                    Never stopped pulsing, the God –
                              kept pushing through the earth like a hand.
What did you say?
                    I knelt upon ashes, numb consonants, the swollen absence
                              shook against my lips. I eat the fulfilled earth. I meant
                              what I said about hunger.
Where were you?
                              In my dream I heard her unlock the last gate. I was
                              looking out from her unlit eyes, gasping.

Was it your blood or hers?
                    The dark is possessive. The dark has always said Mine.

MIKA HORIBUCHI, *7 OF HEARTS*, 2015, OIL ON CANVAS, 24 1/2 x 17 1/2 INCHES. COURTESY THE ARTIST AND ANAT EBGI GALLERY, LOS ANGELES

HELEN CLARK OLDFIELD, *TRIAD (OR THREE)*, 1977. CHARCOAL, INDIA INK HIGHLIGHTED WITH WHITE GOUACHE ON PAPER. 25 x 18 INCHES. FROM *EMERGING FROM THE SHADOWS* (SCHIFFER PUBLISHING).

A Chronology of Scars

Rachel Eliza Griffiths

I don't remember when you began
    in the world. I keep forgetting what word

the water

    made across your tongue. Bent toward

the earth, carved with healing. The trees & animals
pushed into bright air. Ghosts scraped blue rivers

with unknowable depth. Near the skin any blade
or kiss. Near the skin any clock unmaking the ribs

with stone. Even the softest terror breaks
    apart in the fists of our hours. Alone. Yes.

The record will show. Chokecherry leaves ripening
beneath white lashes. The mind of

    the earth turned like a heart after death.

The wound took the form of night.

Which means my naked hand went through
    the bruised dark.

Which says the skin opened without injury.

A woman swells inside mauve fields. A crow
    hushes newborn snow.

A grief makes it own
    blood. The petals beneath me
        have already changed.

The wound gave the night endless

    shame & would not close its mouth.

Rush

J. Malcolm Garcia

Myrtle Avenue, Brooklyn, New York, 2006.

Five boys caged 12 pigeons for two days without food. Then one of the boys carried the pigeons up to the roof of a burned-out apartment building in the projects while the four remaining boys scattered pieces of stale bread in the middle of Myrtle Avenue. When the birds were released, the boys on the avenue crouched, circling into Jet Li *Cradle 2 the Grave* kicks and Tony Jaa *The Protector* kicks as the pigeons dove for the food. They kicked them before they landed and the whole thing grew very loud, and amid a flutter of lightly descending feathers distorted faces shouted out of open windows, snarling for *quiet*! It rained later that afternoon but in the evening the rain stopped, and it got very steamy outside and the stink from the avenue was practically intolerable.

IMAGE: PATRICK JACKSON, *IN HANDS*, 2015. PLASTICINE, POLYURETHANE, EPOXY. 34 x 26 1/2 x 7 1/2 INCHES. COURTESY THE ARTIST AND GHEBALY GALLERY, LOS ANGELES. PHOTO: JEFF MCLANE

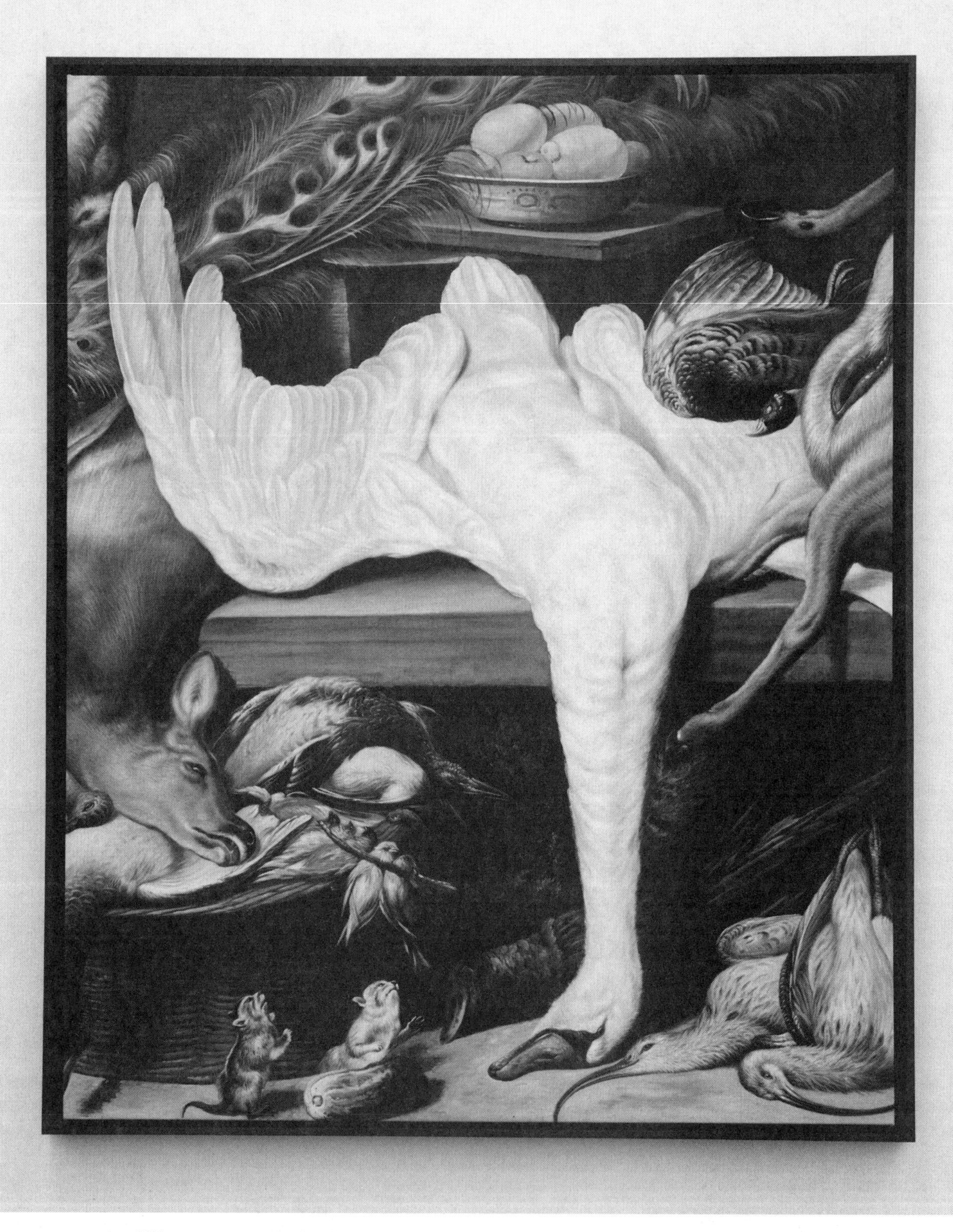

ETHAN COOK, *SWAN*, 2016, OIL ON CANVAS, 62 X 50 INCHES
COURTESY OF THE ARTIST AND ANAT EBGI GALLERY, LOS ANGELES

Spectacle

Anna Rose Welch

There were blessings everywhere.
The man who wouldn't touch me during
or after. The insomnia.
The way my breath sounded leaving,
like teeth into the skin of a fruit.
The heart falls open like a book
when you're brave enough.
As if God had parted you with his own finger.
Even in the dark I can be read
like a shard of bone rejecting its body.
I'm stealing the light from whatever
still has light to give,
which means I wasn't made in the image
of a great darkness capable of swallowing everything.
My mouth is small. My neck can be bent back
like an improperly struck match. Bless me.
Nothing I've built to worship is merciful enough.

In Western Sahara: Inside the 40-Year-Long Military Occupation the World Is Ignoring

Tom Stevenson

THE WESTERN SAHARA is a barren range of areg and hamada decorated by acacia trees and the Harmattan haze, and not much else. It is also the only territory in Africa still subject to settler colonialism. Once a Spanish colony, Western Sahara is now a Moroccan one. Its indigenous people, Hassaniya speakers, who are now known as the Sahrawi, lived for centuries as nomads within a quarter of the Sahara called the khat al-khouf (line of fear) south of the Moroccan sultanate and the Draa River and north of the Mauritanian emirates. Then in 1884 the region was assigned to Spain when the European powers carved up Africa among themselves at the Berlin Conference and it became known as Saguia el Hamra y Río de Oro, or Spanish Sahara. Until the 1940s, the colony of Spanish Sahara was used as a prison for Spanish dissidents.

Under pressure from the UN, Spain eventually gave up its hold on Western Sahara, however the territory was not decolonized. Instead, it was ceded by the Spanish authorities (in violation of international law and against the writ of the International Court of Justice) to Morocco and Mauritania after an impressive coup de théâtre in which 350,000 Moroccans, guarded by thousands of soldiers, were bused over the border to assert Rabat's claim. A week later, at the Madrid Conference in November 1975, the two neighbors agreed to partition the territory and the armies of both countries openly marched in.

The smaller Mauritanian force was quickly beaten back by local resistance, but Morocco fared better: with the help of their air power, the advancing French- and US-backed Moroccan army drove out nearly half of the indigenous Sahrawi, who became refugees in Algeria. Morocco has since introduced thousands of settlers and to this day controls roughly (in all senses of the word) 80 percent of the territory.

Today, Moroccan-occupied Western Sahara is classed as one of the least free places in the world, joining the likes of North Korea, Saudi Arabia, and Syria. In Freedom House's 2015 report, Western Sahara scored -2/40 on political rights, and therefore has the honor of being classed the least free place in the world by that measure. Even Saudi Arabia earned 3/40.

Yet the story of Morocco's invasion and occupation of Western Sahara, and of the regime it runs there, is barely known. Four decades on, the annexation of Western Sahara has elicited almost no outrage. Morocco remains the darling of the US and French business community, and of Washington. The Clintons were recently granted the use of one of the royal palaces while visiting, and the kingdom continues to provide for the West the kind of "security cooperation" in which autocratic monarchies specialize.

In fact, the US-Morocco relationship was strengthened, not threatened, during the invasion of Western Sahara, when the United States worked with France and Saudi Arabia to arm the Moroccan forces, diplomatically support the annexation, and prevent any UN action against it. For 40 years the great powers, including the United States, have collaborated with Rabat, and since the Arab uprisings the West has not only quietly supported Morocco in running its occupation, but held it up as a beacon of reform and moderation in North Africa. Meanwhile the Sahrawi people are divided, but not scattered. More than half live under the harsh Moroccan occupation alongside its settlers, and the remaining refugees live not as a diaspora but in desert refugee camps deep in southern Algeria.

¤

Al-Ayun (also known as Laayoune) is Western Sahara's largest city and the capital of the occupied territory. It is a salmon-colored place that swelled to its current size to house Moroccan settlers in the 1980s and '90s. A small river called the Saqiet al-Hamra (red stream) runs past the city in fits, but few people come by, except to take the bus north for work or visit family and then return. The city bears visible marks of conquest. Its small airport is named after the Moroccan Sultan Hassan I, who never ruled over Western Sahara and died 80 years before the annexation. Al-Ayun Hospital is named with slightly more cause after King Hassan II, who invaded the territory, but the palace seems to be unaware of the irony. It was King Hassan II who in 1961 first formally claimed a right to a "Greater Morocco" that would stretch from the Mediterranean to the Senegal River, including not only Western Sahara, but also all of Mauritania, a large chunk of northern Mali, and western Algeria.

By the early 1970s the palace was forced to abandon its pretensions to all the other territories, but the king vowed never to renounce Western Sahara. The palace's claim is impressed on the city at every opportunity, and with no subtlety. Next to al-Ayun's Boulevard Mohamed V (named after Hassan II's father) lies al-Mechouar square, a large triumphal plaza lined with Moroccan flags and with four otherworldly pillars at its corners. The square is always utterly empty so that one has the vague feeling that walking across it might mean being shot.

Morocco denies that it is occupying Western Sahara at all. When Ban Ki moon described the situation in the territory as an "occupation," Morocco responded by ordering the UN mission in the territory to leave, and at least 73 of the UN's staff were flown out.

It would be difficult to imagine any place that more resembled a military occupation while pretending to be a normal city than al-Ayun. There are scarcely any streets without soldiers or armored vehicles. Estimates of the number of soldiers Morocco has in Western Sahara vary, but usually fall somewhere between 100,000 and 150,000. Even the low estimates are in the tens of thousands, and at any rate you can't turn a corner without seeing evidence of this. The CIA believes the total population of the occupied territory to be around 550,000, but the number of indigenous Sahrawis probably doesn't exceed 160,000. The Moroccan military presence therefore amounts roughly to one soldier for every indigenous Sahrawi. This allows Morocco to dominate the territory and crush dissent. The king's advisors also believe he is safer with most of the troops in Western Sahara than he would be if they were deployed closer to Rabat: a history of coup attempts by the Moroccan army has maintained a healthy fear of the armed forces in the palace.

Along with the soldiers, countless informants and Mukhabarat patrol the streets of Western Sahara's main cities and are responsible for most of the day-to-day surveillance and repression. Groups of spies await the rare arrival of any outsiders in al-Ayun and are on hand to respond if they look as though they might actually talk to any Sahrawi, or at least anyone who is known not to cooperate with the regime. I met some of the spooks while in the city in late 2012. One man in particular was assigned to follow my movements 24 hours a day; he rode a Vespa and slept in the lobby of my hotel. He was no expert, and on one occasion even ducked behind a much too small palm tree in a futile attempt to avoid being spotted.

For the Sahrawis, being followed by the secret police is less amusing, and conditions for dissidents are particularly desperate. There are still small, open protests on the streets, but participants are beaten mercilessly by riot police and plainclothes security officials wielding clubs. Veteran activists bear their scars with pride. Asked whether protesting isn't pointlessly dangerous, they reply: "What else can we do but keep going out to face them?"

When arrested at demonstrations, the dissidents are normally charged with "forming a criminal gang" or "insulting security officers." The prisons are grim places. Morocco was one of the most enthusiastic collaborators in the CIA's rendition and torture program. The techniques used in a secret facility run by the Moroccan intelligence agency, then the Direction de la Surveillance du Territoire (DST) in Temara, near the capital Rabat, are not dissimilar to those still used in the Western Saharan jails. An Amnesty International report earlier this year documented 173 cases of serious torture by the Moroccan state. Many of the targets were Sahrawi. The full panoply of techniques goes from beatings to waterboarding with urine. Most dissidents can name relatives who were either imprisoned and never heard from again or who are still being held.

The early Sahrawi resistance to the occupation was originally formed in 1973 by an armed independence movement known as the Frente Popular de Liberación de Saguía el Hamra y Río de Oro, or Polisario Front, which mounted a series of attacks on Spanish positions and soon won popular support. The movement put up armed resistance to the Moroccan invasion and subsequent 15 years of occupation until the UN brokered a ceasefire in 1991. But there isn't much affection in al-Ayun for the UN peacekeeping mission known as MINURSO, which was the only consistent international presence until its recent ejection. Its staff witnessed the many abuses dealt to the Sahrawi but had no mandate from the Security Council to monitor offenses, let alone prevent them. The mission was established with a view to an internationally monitored referendum in 1992 in which the Sahrawi would decide Western Sahara's fate. The stated goal was de-colonization to be resolved on the basis of the exercise of the right to self-determination by the population of the territory. The UN failed in that task after a campaign by Morocco to include thousands of its own citizens in the voter list. The UN eventually rejected 93 percent of the more than 99,000 prospective voters from Morocco sponsored by Rabat, but the verification process took years, and by 2000 the UN had lost its enthusiasm for the referendum, leaving MINURSO in an awkward position.

For the first fifteen years of MINURSO's existence, a Moroccan flag flew over its headquarters in al-Ayun. The mission's diplomats had protested from the start that flying either party's flag was a surrender of UN neutrality, but the flag remained until the morning of October 3, 2006, when the Danish General Kurt Mosgaard, who was temporary acting head of MINURSO, finally took it down. "I had expected to be sacked," he told me. "The complaints went directly from Morocco to the UN, to the ambassador and the highest level, but somehow I survived." The Moroccan authorities were furious; having failed to get Mosgaard fired, they responded by hoisting dozens of Moroccan flags to surround the MINURSO compound. To this day one cannot approach the UN headquarters without noticing the sea of Moroccan red around it.

Poor and arid though it appears, Western Sahara is not entirely devoid of spoils. In 1947, near the town of Bou Craa, Spanish geologist Manuel Alía Medina discovered one of the largest deposits of high-grade phosphate in the world and reported his findings directly to Franco. By the early 1960s the colonial authorities were exploiting the deposits. After annexation Morocco acquired the mines, and today the state company Office Chérifien des Phosphates controls both Morocco's domestic industry and the colonial reserves. It is now the largest phosphate producer in the world. The UN's legal experts concluded in 2008 that Moroccan exploitation of any Western Saharan resources, including phosphates, was illegal unless approved of by the Sahrawi. However the UN's legal findings have made little difference: last year 2.1 million tons of phosphate rock were shipped from Western Sahara to Vancouver, New Zealand, Australia, India, Venezuela, Lithuania, and the United States.

Phosphates, and the fishing and offshore oil exploration that Morocco manages in Western Sahara, all entrench the annexation and allow Morocco to recoup some of the costs of military occupation. Morocco may have spent as much as $2.5 billion on infrastructure in the territory, most of it on military bases, prisons, and surveillance. Perhaps the greatest expense was building, maintaining, and manning the massive sand wall that divides the occupied territory and the slender remains of the Western Saharan desert under Polisario's control. The wall was built during the war in an effort to counter an effective guerrilla army. Raiding was the established form of combat for the Sahrawi, who knew the land and how to avoid pitched battles, and for the first few years of the conflict did well. They trounced the Mauritanian army and embarrassed the Moroccans. The war turned against Polisario in 1981, when the wall went under construction. By 1987 it covered 1,600 miles — a remarkable feat, though aside from some roads and prisons Morocco hasn't built much since. Not much is left to Polisario in the way of "liberated territory," about 20 percent of the total, most of it useless, with no access to the coast, and much of it sown with landmines.

Walking through al-Ayun, where the ratio of settlers to indigenous Sahrawis is high, you still see Sahrawi deraa robes and hear Hassaniya spoken. The Moroccan regime usually denies — or better, erases — the existence of a Sahrawi people in the ethnic and nationalist sense. It insists that people south of the Tarfaya Strip are simply southern Moroccans, living in the nation's "Southern Provinces." But the Sahrawi in this part of the territory are still adamant that it is theirs and are struggling to decide the fate of their country behind the backs of the military and security apparatus.

East of the wall, life is different. When the refugees fled the advance of the Moroccan army in 1975 they coalesced in two groups in the eastern settlements of Guelta Zemmur and Oum Dreyga. The Moroccan air force bombed both towns and hit the refugee column with ordnance and napalm, so Polisario fighters led the refugees across the border and up into the Algerian Sahara south of Tindouf. The refugees in the sprawling camps can access the parts of Western Sahara that Morocco doesn't occupy, but there is nothing aside from inhospitable desert and a dusting of land mines. The refugees were half — or more accurately two-fifths — of an entire people forced to start from scratch on a thankless stretch of land. Measles killed many in the first year, and no concerted international aid arrived until 1977. Since then they have been living mostly on UN aid. Today there are five camps south of Tindouf. All but one bear the names of the cities of Western Sahara: Laayoune, Smara, Dakhla, Aousserd, and Boujdour.

Flying to the camps gives no proper sense of their remoteness. If you traveled overland from Oran you would first cross two ranges, the Tell and Saharan Atlas, and proceed through a series of forgettable towns. Eventually the settlements would all but run out, and the desert would begin. After Béchar you would not see much save 500 miles of sand and rock. The last stop before Tindouf would be Oum El Assel, "mother of honey," where there wouldn't be any bees. Having reached Tindouf there would still be a drive of several hours before you made it to Dakhla, the farthest of the camps. A goat pen built of rusted metal doors announces the approach to al-Ayun camp. Their numbers may not be as high as the Polisario Front claims, but there are likely more than 100,000 Sahrawi living in the camps. For the last 40 years they have maintained a complex cultural and social life, based on a template of a post-independence society.

Morocco and its supporters, including a lobby in Washington worth millions of dollars and led by a group called the "Moroccan American Center for Policy," claim that the Polisario has no popular legitimacy within the camps, and in extreme cases that it is jailing the refugees in open-air prisons run by the Polisario and Algeria — described almost as Saharan equivalents of Chacabuco, General Augusto Pinochet's concentration camp in the Atacama Desert.

A recent report from Human Rights Watch meticulously investigated Morocco's accusations about the camps and found almost every claim was either completely false or exaggerated beyond recognition. The camps are sometimes even referred to as "terrorist recruiting grounds," a bizarre claim easily belied by visiting them. The camps are constantly host to aid agencies, including Oxfam and the UNHCR, as well as international observers, all of whom have curiously failed to notice that they are working in terrorist recruitment grounds. The claim had its dubious foundation in the kidnapping of three European humanitarian aid workers in 2011, when armed al-Qaeda–linked fighters attacked one of the refugee camps, taking the workers hostage and injuring a Sahrawi guard.

The camps are neither terrorist centers nor prisons, but the difficulty of the conditions is hard to overstate. For a start there is simply nothing to do. Life is a grinding, monotonous struggle of boredom and lentils. The aid that comes through has been cut in the last few years, and the refugees now get a great deal of their calories from granulated sugar. A large family told me they go through 50 kilograms of it every 25 days. It is not a life to which anyone would aspire. The Algerian Sahara is a fierce place, and one quickly gets the feeling that behind the resolve the refugees do harbor a feeling of having been condemned. If they are condemned, it is at the hand of the Moroccan occupation and not at that of their own leadership or Algeria, whatever ulterior motives the latter doubtless has in supporting and sheltering the refugees.

The refugees have been in the camps for 40 years; one soon notices that there are plenty of buildings. The Smara camp has now taken on the appearance of a small city in itself. In all camps there are communal buildings for local organizing and public gatherings in which the refugees get together to trade stories about the atrocities of the annexation. The nomad tents are still there, every family must have one, but time and prudence mean the Sahrawi refugees in all camps have built brown box-shaped huts made of sand and water bricks around them. When the sandstorms come they are of great use so long as the roofs are not blown off. The huts are not exactly pictures of permanence. They have no foundations, and when heavy rains came last summer the water just washed hundreds of them away.

¤

A cemetery lies near the center of Dakhla camp. A small wall partly conceals its graves, marked not with headstones but stone shards arranged in circles around the buried bodies. The markers of the dead are visible on the walk through the camp, a constant reminder of those who died before returning to their homes. The same stone circles are used by the Sahrawi to mark land mines in the 20 percent of Western Sahara that is not occupied by Morocco. The cemeteries are also partly filled by landmine victims, and the mines are still killing and maiming. Fourteen were seriously injured by them last year, their legs blown off in some cases, and two were killed. Few Sahrawi still live as nomads in their strip of land because of the mines, and for those who brave them, the costs are high. For a nomadic family the loss of even a single camel or goat is a serious blow, and "dozens of dozens" of livestock are killed every year.

The Polisario's prime minister in exile, Abdelkader Taleb Omar, describes the camps as partly a "permanent protest" against the occupation of Western Sahara. But if you want to hold a permanent protest, the remote Sahara, more than a thousand miles from the nearest neutral capital city, is hardly the best place. Omar is aware of this, but if the refugees were simply to disperse, Morocco's hand would be greatly improved, and this they won't accept. The existence of the camps makes it difficult to close the book on the conflict and accept the annexation as an immutable fact of history.

"Nothing stays the same," Omar told me. "This is how we were educated." But younger refugees, prone to despair and anger, say they would sooner die than keep waiting.

"Nothing ever changes," one of the more embittered young Sahrawi said. "The UN come here in their nice clothes and they don't even speak to us, as if we're dirty. We've had enough. I was born here and I don't want to die here — I want to fight." But a Sahrawi assault on the wall would be suicide, and even if a refugee force armed with decades-old weaponry got through the minefields and defensive lines, the Moroccan army would make quick work of them.

The Polisario foreign minister Mohamed Salem Ould Salek, whose parents and two sisters were "disappeared" by Moroccan forces, is charged with leading the diplomatic assault. He still insists that the goal is the implementation either of the original UN referendum plan or what's known as "Baker II," a compromise UN special envoy James Baker proposed in 2003 — which the Polisario, then Morocco, subsequently rejected — in which the refugees would return and live autonomously under Moroccan rule for five years, after which a referendum on independence would finally be held. "The main obstacle is France," Ould Salek says. Despite a recent chill in relations — the Moroccans rashly tortured two French-born detainees — France remains Morocco's single largest trading partner, arms supplier, and inward investor, with around 750 corporate subsidiaries in the country, and sends more than three million tourists every year. Having rejected Baker II, Morocco launched its autonomy proposal, which dispenses with the idea of a referendum and proposes the Sahrawi return to Western Sahara as an autonomous region under Moroccan rule. The plan has the tentative backing of France and the United States but has been rejected outright by the Sahrawi, who see it as an attempt to strip them of their right to self-determination.

Why should anyone care? Western Sahara is an out-of-the-way place, far from the centers of world power and the prizes for which those powers play, and it's in Africa, no less. At least that seems to be the logic. The UN Security Council has limited itself to the role of a broker, making encouraging noises and sponsoring negotiations, as hostile parties try to reach a modus vivendi. It hasn't worked, and the great powers have done nothing to rectify the situation.

The bigger problem is that the positions of Morocco and the Sahrawi are entirely irreconcilable. No amount of talks will change that. King Mohammed VI has made it clear that Morocco will not give up Western Sahara "until the end of time." There is no reason to believe he isn't serious. Official US policy is to treat Morocco's 2007 autonomy plan as "serious and credible," but a program called "advanced regionalization," signaled by the king in 2011, would now devolve administrative powers to all of Morocco's provinces, beginning with the "Southern Provinces" to which Western Sahara de facto belongs.

The intention appears to be to bury any notion of a "special status" for the territory: the proposals admit no area or region called Western Sahara, and only one of the three provinces involved is entirely on Western Saharan land. The other two combine parts of Western Sahara with parts of Morocco. Washington may be impressed by the idea of autonomy as a solution, but Morocco no longer looks to be offering it.

The reality is that Western Sahara has never been a local conflict, and isn't now. It was partly born from European colonialism, and continued with crucial aid from France, the United States, and Saudi Arabia, under Cold War auspices, which allowed Morocco to check Polisario's military initiatives and then go on to annex the land.

Insisting today that Morocco and the Sahrawi negotiate a settlement while knowing that their positions are irreconcilable and that Morocco is the more powerful party amounts to de facto support for annexation. To actually solve the problem, the world — in practice, the powerful nations, including the United States, who are currently opposing a good part of the world — would have to force one of the parties to do something it does not want to do. Specifically, it would mean dealing with a king who would take any challenge to his power in Western Sahara as a personal and hereditary affront.

The burden falls on France and the United States especially, if there is any genuine respect for a world built on equal laws, to do something different — to take responsibility, or simply some interest, in a distant corner of Africa. ❖

Aubade

Joanna Klink

NOT EVEN ALIVE in
departing. The rush of
strong dark current

through these trees,
muscle-flickers of shade –
the lavish announcements
of

summer stilled to a
moment then dis-
missed, as if it could

all happen again, only
better. Fresh and

sorrowless. Is it
mistrust of the future or

panic that makes us
insist on a dream at the
expense of what is.

The world you imagine
would never leave you.

But the rain that may
blacken over a coast in
hanging clouds we are

miles from feels deeply
real. As does the light

folding through
maples right by your
door, in white liquid curves.

·:·

AN OLD SINKING COUCH,
another toothbrush,
a question about

dinner. Everyday
things suddenly un-
nerved – a habit of

distance so fixed and deep
you use the same
words you used

years ago. It takes
all the time we have to
make
sense of each other.

Why not new words?
Why the same blank thirst
solved with the exact same

reach of your hand?
Is this truly what you mean?

To leave, because you love
life? Or because
you loved badly?

·:·

EARLY DARK outside your
house. A reading light
inside. Before I ever

entered and threw my
arms around your son,
there were two homes, two

kitchens, films coffee and
books, a necklace
laced silver with wood, overly

elaborate complications,
willingness without
permission, desire

with no course, the absence
of rancor, an absence

of defeat, botched
gifts, snow on the hills
(those are small white

flowers), winters, not waking
early, informed really of

nothing, fearful, careful
never to resemble a family,
admiration, un-

moved disregard, thoughts
about oneself – we
went on – until I

was the only one who
knew, pressing my
fingers again and again

into my eyes. Have you,
like me, felt life
drained from you

by someone you tried
so hard to love?
Should it ever take such

effort? Whether you
move, whether you stay,
you have lived here a

while. And burn
in the spring dusk,
if you can bear it.

ADA MAY SHARPLESS, *PASTORALE*, C. 1926, PLASTER CAST SCULPTURE WITH GOLD PAINTED FINISH, 9 1/2 x 26 x 6 1/2 INCHES, FROM *EMERGING FROM THE SHADOWS* (SCHIFFER PUBLISHING).

Bad Review

(Death/Rash/Envy/Eggs/Uncle/Therapy/Aversion/Sidekick/Rush/Panic/Corruption/Alphabet/Tattoo/Digits/Lemon/Double/Teeth)

Rebecca McClanahan

An Open Letter to a Fellow Writer Who Has Just Received His First Bad Review

As if you wanted to *receive* it, as if it were a gift. Strange, the words we use for such things, words like "his book, which has just been *released*," as if the book committed a crime it has recently served time for.

Yes, I know it hurts, but remember, this is not death, though it will feel like it for a while. Don't panic, don't do something rash. Try to calm yourself if you can because therapy is expensive, plus it takes up time, precious time that you need for writing the next book.

But okay, if therapy is necessary, go for aversion therapy. Sniff some rotten eggs, then open the review pages and keep doing this — rotten eggs, review pages — until the two sensations become one. Or until, together, they add up to something you never want to go near again: eggs + reviews = corruption. This will keep you from reading the reviews, thus saving yourself for the real work you need to do.

Whatever it takes, try to avoid envy, even if, side by side on the same journal pages, the book of your closest friend, your sidekick, garners critics' praise. Envy has teeth. It bites anything in its way, and its bite stings like lemon on a paper cut. You know about paper cuts — you're a writer! Paper cuts and words sting. Sometimes the words are true, and truth stings the most. But remember, that's their job, these critics, to tell their own truth. Some are good at it — their words are a gift you gladly receive because they teach you about your work; others rush to judgment, make terrible errors; and some, it is clear, never even read your book, giving another meaning to "a bad review."

You will feel this way for a while. But not forever. Go into hiding for a few days if you must. Indulge in your favorite joy: salsa, on the dance floor or with your chips; the freckles across your grandson's nose; single-malt scotch. Cry if you want. Then go back to the desk, trying to call forth something, anything, to kick-start the alphabet that is still ticking inside you. It doesn't take much: an overheard conversation, the lint on your jacket, the uncle you haven't thought of for years. Remember the tattoo on his left bicep, the double row of digits adding up to, well, you were never sure what they added up to, but that's not the point. The point is, he believed in those digits. He wore them with pride, rolling his sleeve high to bare them even to strangers, because they told a story only he could tell.

The Great American Songbook

David Biespiel

West End Blues

WE WILL ARISE and live inside future wars, Winston Churchill says in 1925, that will be even less romantic and picturesque. We will be a war, not of armies, but of whole populations, and be exposed, Winston Churchill says, to mass destruction by lethal vapor, and that even the gardener will exterminate the wasp nest with the right poison after measuring the exact amount to put it stealthily in the right place at the right time. Entire communities will be destroyed, Winston Churchill says, and not one wasp will get near enough to sting the gardener. But he will not regard the gardener as a hero — thus in accents, in parchment, myths fade into a 12-bar blues. Do you know the name of the gardener now or whether his eyes are bulging or soft? Or what purpose his hands have meant? Do you see him masquerade as a clown? Or a flagrant, broken butcher who tells jokes to the crocus bulbs with his red kerchief tied behind his neck and dripping with the sweat of anger? Death, then — is it said and done like a cyst, a sequence of ministering to anecdote, or antidote to a silent dip of morning crossing the miles of causeway to Lake Pontchartrain past the green orphan inches where everything is preserved beneath a lacquer of sunlight? It is pleasing, Winston Churchill says, to look back over the plains and morasses through which our path has lain in the past, and remember in tradition the great years of pilgrimage. Now: Do you notice the crows lifting above the southbound lights to the lake like mass effects in modern life? Or west of there, the way over the bridges, driving past the ringing refineries that exhale zeroes into the dark world where oil burns with the cat's eyes of pot deals and hash hits, past the sand and clay layers of Humble Oil in Baytown and the ghost of Spindletop in Beaumont, past lunch pail, past soiled shoes, past Lake Charles and its average morning humidity of 90 percent, past Jeff Davis Parish which requires no explication, all of it reclaiming some lost checkpoint of flame or shades of wind the color of gunmetal, bad farms and the glamour of swamps? It's not meticulous country down there, shadowed with rough, and shadowed with sad, and shadowed with hurricanes that drop into Port Arthur — Betsy and Rita, Humberto and Edouard and Ike — without any recess from the myths about backwoods and narrow stairs and a father hushed over a jam-jar-sized glass of milk. — I must have noticed one crow, at least, on that drive, must have noticed two crows and a thrush. I must have noticed even with my one eye swelled from so many years elsewhere, swelled as an oyster shell swells without luster or witness or the blossom and blush of withered berries. Those petals are now beginning to discolor toward the slum edges of autumn, discolor and wobble, naturally, and obscured, half in song and half, as reported, in warble.

Surfin' USA

Except for the old dog under my foot and the early shadows of summer, except for the thaw in the oceans and the bushy blonde wind, we are settling in all over on this bank of the city — though by the time anyone sees us through the leafage and leaf rot, through the routes they've taken and the disappearances, through the aromas coming off the waters, drifting past like a summer stepping out of fire — except for all that — we wouldn't know how to smoke out the wives who have disappeared and the husbands who've died. Though there on the clothesline are his striped shirts and his boots by the back stoop of Del Mar — if his boots fit, anyone of us could stroll out in them before too late at dawn for a taste of beer and curse the foam and the inky drifts, the bridges, the reefs, the men in the water, and the women sleeping at the edge of the county line where the last of the tall weeds are waxed down. This looks to be Del Mar alright! Here we grew out our hair and fiddled with death, ecstasy got distilled in the rise to our feet, the tube times broke over the back, and the small swells from the south thrashed into boundlessness, and therefore the breakers closed out and our breathing got mangy, sometimes trashy, and sometimes sweet, sick, or silky, or crisp, or soft as a shell. We'd slide atop the hard swells and the sky would fade and the waters would move beneath our chests. And the clouds pass by and the birds cry as they passed overhead. All of it like the inside-outside rhythm of a heart, deep in pieces, trembling in the divinity of, I hate to say, escape and submission. When John F. Kennedy says, The path we have chosen for the present is full of hazards as all paths are, he means that the cost of freedom is high. We have paid it, John F. Kennedy says, but one path we shall never choose, and that is the path of surrender, or submission. Though Simone Weil says, Oppression that is clearly inexorable and invincible does not give rise to revolt but to submission. And yet, all that time alone in the turtle hour and with the air cool, we see the birds diving like mist into the water, with the first light catching the first waves — all that time paddling out into the salt of yearning. Therefore, suddenly, we settle into the barrels against the round sun beyond the dying night fires and the untroubled sand, settle out there into the first, low, scallop shapes of waves until we can stare back at the weak light in the far western edge, settle in, O, untethered land.

Summertime

If I were to pick one season to love it would be summer with its rooster mornings and sliced artichokes that turn sparrows to lullabies. It's then I can stare at the eyes of the roses and keep still and not know what discretion is needed to enter the florets in a missing pair of work gloves. Not one daddy is a rich man in my city though I sit for hours listening to the birds take quick and crazy to the sky. That's how we know this corner of the mouth or that habit kept secret. Even Saint Peter cannot see it from a thousand miles above high cotton with the lights up and twinkling forth. In the year 1880, Thom. Edison's patent drawing for the improvement in electric lamps shows the glass envelope and the coiled filament with its notion of connection and civic fire, but not the inert gasses at low pressure that becomes the stretched out high note of the USA. Though here, now, may I draw your attention to Figure Three where the light is going to rise up swinging — with the head of the filament like a minuteman with his powdered wig and revolution, and the side curls of the filament like the hair of an immigrant Jew, and the white thin collar of the filament, too, like a fisted priest in contemplation, and the long arms of the filament like a slave woman's arms and a slave master's, and the artificial legs of the filament — those are the legs of the amputated warrior. What lullaby will comfort the base and the connecting wire of the states to rise up swinging and spread its wings and take to the sky? Till that morning comes, only I will remember the empty crossroad where the melodies of summer were born in some young body in the middle of America where the snows came down in Yiddish flakes and a single peddler below used to hum — Oi Khodyt Son Kolo Vikron — Lullaby, oh lullaby — Oi, yiddle, yiddle, oi, yiddle — at the dining room table next to his new pals Irving and Max and Sheldon and Ira and Sol which is short for Solomon which is American for Shlomo. The fellas from Des Moines and Brooklyn and Miami and Houston where they would gather mornings for round-the-clock specials and famous sandwiches — broiled genuine calf liver steak with onions, cold boiled chicken with sliced tomatoes, corned beef, pickled tongue, cervelat, knockwurst, kreplach soup, hot cabbage borscht with half a potato, cheese blintzes with chicken livers on toast. From everywhere in America now I can look out over the highest oak and beyond into the fresh Republican miles with all the crazy deprivations and corn-fed sinners fanning themselves against mosquitoes and the dead-stop wind off the Mississippi. It's no use loving a season. No. So, hush. Hush. Little baby, it's always been this way, over and over, even if hearts seem more coarse, and mothers and fathers stand by the days' little seconds and ships of light, and the gardens are cutting up with yellow squash and cherry tomatoes. Even now I want to chitter at this wind and wake up with a new light on my face as it makes catfish diamonds on the walls, and drink cold coffee from a short mug, and study the curiosity of sparklers and pinwheels of the wildflower and showers of cosmos, and roses in the sky, fountains of starlight and hop-hop of thunder — with whistling for sleep, with the feathers and pearls of dreamers, and the distant whimpers and whispers of the beloved that become the coronet souls of green leaf and high grass, and the first bars are hummed above the cities — Ba-de-baaaaah, ba-de-dah-de-de-dap, daaah, Baaaaah-de-dap-dap-daaah, bah-de-da-de-daaaahh-dah. Baaaaah-de-dap-dap-daaaah, Bah-de-dop-dop-de-doppen-a-dah-la-la-la, Bah-dop-de-de-dop-dop, dop-deeeh-dah-de-dah-daaah.

Son of a Preacher Man

If I told you that once I read in *Time* magazine the name of a boy I knew who used his constitutional rights to shoot himself in the head over a breakup with a girl, you'd say, not that I was making it up, but that you know someone who once took you by the hand and led you into the soft-pistol dusk where nothing could reach you. That kid was 17, and seemed, I admit, to be going nowhere, as if walking the north road out of town alongside the night train rippling over to Quebec. Here, it's July. The corn is gathering round in fine, dark, green tassels and clusters that I will not touch for fear of losing, not far off, their earlier shadows, although the grass is ablaze too and isn't easy to whistle with. I believe I can hear him singing, maybe, of rain. And listening, maybe, to the river. And smoking a joint. The green light of summer slowly grazing the oncoming darkness. The high filling his hair like a dream of a bright world that sparks up the rows of houses. And them houses, one and the same, burning smoke up into the proof of unharmed night, untouched night. The boy walks like a small creature along the path side of the river, and not a logjam to be seen — I must tell you: the other side of the river is where Henry Thoreau in 1856 hiked the Table Rock outcropping on Fall Mountain, hiked up the glittered gravel under the loose hawks overhead but not under the new power lines, hiked past the moosewood's green bark and the witch hazel, the beech and birch trees, and down below, the clock tower's chime like the echo of a creaky fan shuddering across the two towns. If I told you why we came there, you would not ask about the long days and the heaving summers and the small bellows of desire the land makes. A breath comes and goes, comes and goes, that's all. And the sky passes overhead in streaks of unmarred stars. No trouble to be seen. But it isn't always easy, the days and nights filtering the hiss of dinnertime with a phone ringing in a distant room — and no one answering. And I may have to invent you to read this, to remember that boy as I have, his high forehead and sweet voice, the mood in his eyes like that of a lost cat, a name like Nate. But I will try to make you like me as I tell you all this, both of us wanderers who favor the river towns with their split personalities and shared graduation days, and the motel bars with their unnoticed dreamers drifting by after the dogs have strayed — and where the words for desire, for forgiveness, for waking to kisses on the cheek are held in the breath and are a gift. And the meaning of sleep is not easily understood. Sleep that drifts as the tongues of boats drift on the river with the assurance of a swirling wind. Lord knows, I have not washed my face, nor saved kernels for a new planting, nor written his full name in black ink. My handwriting is like that of a boy's anyway — dark gazelles of letters with the bolts and crosses of the past. When you turn over the card onto which I must now scrawl his name, you will not find blood or bullets or wine, or even winter, not here, where the wind is like the sly quiet of time. His name is like the way we hunger, you and I, or the you I have made you into, to remember the words we have spoken to those who have died, hunger for the phone to ring and for someone with a familiar voice like smoke-filled air that comes and goes on the wings of sparrows — we hunger for someone like that, we hunger for him to lift up the receiver and answer it.

Jambalaya (On the Bayou)

Sometimes in midsummer I come to understand the proverb that a gem cannot be polished without friction, and that filet gumbo is rooted as much in bark as it is in death, and that the hard, glossy, secret flight of the afterlife is with you every day — just as the asphalt farm-to-market roads are, just as the fruit jars are, and the wild hogs, and the built-out places. That's why if I had learned something all those years ago about history I might have known that in all matters of opinion our adversaries are insane. This fruit fly on the underside of my arm seems aware, if that's what it is, of the predicament, twitching like an impatient knitter who has not given up on Allah and who will not speak about the sweetest dark that clots the land like one who will not give up on the spirit of the divine. So who does not wonder what to make of days like this one, when anyone seeking a sky that's blank as words must believe in a borrowed primitivism kept in the pockets of old fathers, folded as clouds are folded, but un-crimped too, for the sake of a secret. There's an air of mystery to that sort of secret, like a sky discarded out of its mirror, leading us falsely to a strange wish we might free ourselves with. Or else: The clouds recruit the hours to come in early with my machazomio! — As in winter, cleaned up and edged-out, I can touch that adversary like braille, and the years won't harden or fit inside a palm. Even now, until I turn toward the big river, I will wait here, ready to be resurrected, heaving my spirit into the black dust and the pollen and the shriveling whistles of the damned, and I will bathe in the big fun waters, and we'll go one, two, three, four, five six, seven, eight, nine, Baby, I'm so glad you are mine. Two. Four. Six. Eight. Ten. Baby, please, don't leave me again. We'll go like that, and the freakish belief of a soul lighter than a shadow will drift away like absentmindedness, but not like romance, not like soft voices on the back porches of July. We'll go now, speaking without harm, speaking low, low, and close to the ear.

As Time Goes By

Don't ask me why the street ran this way and not the other way. From Brownsville north to Hartford the road is called the Hartford Road. From Hartford south to Brownsville the road is called the Brownsville Road. The asphalt holds both light and darkness, and, going both ways, the road is like a tawny river to which the villagers come with their oxen and begin to plant seed into the dirt. I've sat in the town square at midday and looked across the low banks and not known how to name the birds. I called them unknown birds and had not realized my duty to them, nor to the trees in which they alighted. Just the same, I could not deny the multitudes on the sidewalks, the faces and shapes and bodies I have not yet invited home or lamented over, not yet been aware of the harm done to, but stood alongside with my ladder and clippers. And yet, still: Do my hands have a memory of their hands? Even museums hold time in their little objects. The world will always welcome shame and myth, and journeys to acquaint yourself with districts and provinces, with hills and groves, knowing that this lilac bush and that oak, or that moving target of footsteps, or this alley that came into being before we existed will remain when we are the dust. Do not ask, who will lay down their arms and who will march in your parade with balloons and dance with the cyclist and his fife. I do not envy them. Nor the drummer, nor the martial artists, because here is a school band in stirrups and red helmets high-stepping like a day's glitter. And here too: So many slick marionettes. And no princess on the balcony, what with the conquerors having swirled, like gilded children, from the long war toward home, dragging — as the wind drags — behind their aging mothers.

Blitzkrieg Bop

You believe God is in the wind and spinning the late leaves over the heads of the buttercups. But take this single rose or these blossoms on the low bushes — they seem to ask you to pick them and scatter them across the city as you walk among the birds like a bird yourself, twittering on your toes in a straight line with little difference between your life and theirs, drinking the same luscious water from the pink and white feeders and the crazy cracks in the ground as they do, touching the grass and letting your body fall, where if you could pull the roots, you'd feel as if you were touching whatever is left of the sunshine on the earth. No, this is not a time for all that — life is too "Hey Ho," is it not? Once, in the dark: I remembered to lock the door. But whether I was on the inside or the outside of the door, I don't remember, as I don't remember writing to you, "Never seek the wind in the field. It is useless to try and find what is gone." — I do remember the taste of the glue on the envelope, the bitter taste on my tongue which must be what those who perfect war know about murdering a man, shooting the bullet between the lumbar and the sacrum as if between truth and loneliness. A man who once said this to his girl lives on the street one over from her father's house. And he said, too: "Don't forget me," with a voice that was part blood in the mouth and part red sky. And she hasn't as she hasn't forgotten the stars or the sea or the wind that whips and dozes and drifts above thick grass, as she hasn't forgotten slowly to climb into bed years after years later, long after he said, "don't forget me," because slowness is what the soft dirt does. Slowness is what's left inside the old rattle. Slowness is lying face up in the snow. It's what she keeps to herself. What she returns to. It's one thing no one else has.

Magic Carpet Ride

When they found me after the war I'd been dancing like a dog into the trees and was drifting as if my legs were broken and my arms open wide, and the stars far off. It must have looked as if I were welcoming what we can see in the moments we awaken. As when the arms come back to your sides and your eyes close, and there is little triumph, but you're breathing okay, and the sounds of your body rage against the lousy world — and the sun blinks out its exaltations and shines up the street as the rows of dogs head home without one salt stick to chew on. That's when you think it best to walk down to the river like a prisoner who gives two thoughts to the weeds and the fur on the goats and the wet fields, who thinks about blood and the nausea of graves. And thinks this too: The ride is like the way heroin flashes. And all laments of the old blow like pollen. So that even if you have drunk blood, you will still know sweetness, still know how the wings of a bird work above the bridges and the furrows of the centuries. I'm like all that now, rotting in my suit and bearded face, leaning against a small fence because this is the mad

ZACHARY LEENER, *FIVE ETCHINGS (SKYSCRAPER)*, 2015, SOFTGROUND, DRYPOINT, SPITBITE, AQUATINT, 16 1/4 x 13 INCHES
EDITION OF 10 (3 AP). COURTESY THE ARTIST AND TIF SIGFRIDS GALLERY, LOS ANGELES.

hour where the sound of bugs eating up the leaves takes you away. On this ride, it goes likes this: when you surround yourself with porches and an empty chair, when you inflame your eyes and gasp for the wildness and sob over the bodies of doves, and even if you've never saved a life, you don't know what you'll find between fire and the mountains. Could be the senator dead on the floor of the Ambassador Hotel kitchen, and the war still going on with its buried shells. Could be the mouths of the newly born with their charms and sorrows. Could be a wolf running alone in a meadow in the twilight, a clock stirring in a dream, babbling about history. You could find all that down by the exhausted river like a side road leading to another side road, like, there, a blue jay vanishing under a lift bridge, leaving this kingdom for some other, and therefore you understand that it does not set you free, and still you don't know what you can see.

Proud Mary

I know Mary is nothing if not suicidal. She hitches her garter like a bride, and tonight has found the shrubs for a place to bed down under — with an eight ball for a pillow — somewhere behind the Irish pub we stumbled out of, sore as horses, missing the ditch by a step. This summer the trees started nice and easy and have ended nice and rough. This summer the trees have hives of silence. They give off a light under which a crowd can croon. The leaves are like confetti, the leaves are like a patch of bells. Even the riverboat queens applaud their greeny societies that have nothing to do with the closing of hands or a body abandoned to the night. Just now, after the casualty notification process is over, the neighborly policemen come by and rub their night sticks into the hours of the wind. They don't worry about the way things might have been. When they watch the flies buzz, they do not know one Mary from another — Mary the right hand pilot, or Mary on the whale boat, Mary in silence or Mary at the altar, Mary the virgin or Mary the child riding her unicycle, turning her big wheel, or Mary the lunatic in the asylum, Mary the machinist who winks at moths and fish eggs, Mary the gatekeeper who completes the race and leans on her rifle and takes her position. Mary who comes in from the sugar field. Mary who lies awake listening to the rain's own gods. Mary who shuts her eyes. Mary who keeps time for the band. Mary the convert who sings out to all of them in single file, shining their torches above the fish in the river. — And now if I sleep, I must choose, America, between the 10,000 Marys. But I mustn't lose a minute of sleep about the way things might have been. No, not for Mary, mother of Jesus, or Mary, sister of Moses, Mary of Bethany or Mary of Clopas, Mary Richards, or Mary Poppins who keeps on turning, keeps on burning, rolling on the river. ❖

Death

Suzanne Berne

In that part of Virginia, so close to Manassas and Bull Run, most of the big old houses were haunted. A secret stair lifted up or maybe a trapdoor disappeared within a foyer's complicated parquet floor. In my grandmother's house, two hinged panels in the casing around the living room doorjambs had once concealed rifles and the front hall closet had a false back.

A contractor bought the house from my father in the late '80s. Not long ago I drove down from Washington after spending a couple days with my grown son, with whom I am not close, but some things should be said in person. In the same way, I thought I'd like to see the old house.

I parked in the courtyard, got out of the car, and straightened my jacket. A woman opened the front door and after I introduced myself, she let me look around downstairs.

The breakfast room still had its bluestone floor, and French doors in the dining room still opened onto the verandah and a view of the lawn and pastures and hills. The rest of the house had been gutted. And the smell was gone. That old smell of dry wood and stone and gravy and fireplace ash.

The woman had not known about the hinged panels or the closet. As she and I walked through the dining room, I told her how every so often my grandmother would invite a few of her friends to lunch and afterward they would sit over pie and coffee, telling stories.

For instance, there was often one of waking in the night to piano music.

"The Spanish Waltz," a mild thin voice would insist, "as clear as I am talking to you now."

Everyone would rustle their napkins, looking out at the sunlit lawn beyond the verandah as the room darkened and lavender shadows stretched under the creamer and china coffee pot and across the white tablecloth, and then someone else would cough politely and describe cigar smoke wafting through a house where no one smoked cigars, or a bathtub faucet that turned on by itself.

Until finally, saved for last, someone would offer a story about a face glimpsed in the window of an empty upstairs room.

A woman's face, usually. Pale, with an urgent look. "Like she was trying to tell us something." And the very next day a young cousin, or someone's brother, or an aunt who was visiting, precipitously died.

"And from that day on," the storyteller would say, "anybody who sleeps in that room feels a chill in the night, even if it's August and hot enough to melt a brick."

I felt that chill myself, recalling those whispery, confiding, gratified old voices.

The woman said ghosts were part of the charm of an old house. I said she was exactly right; they were just another kind of company, with their Spanish waltzes and cigar smoke, and no sense feeling haunted when we've all got a secret panel somewhere. She glanced a second time at her watch, so I thanked her for letting me stop by.

At the front door she asked if I had a long trip ahead.

"Not that long," I said.

As I got in my car, I glanced at the upstairs windows and gave them a nod.

Thank you to *LARB*'s Board of Directors

ALBERT LITEWKA
REZA ASLAN
BILL BENENSON
LEO BRAUDY
BERT DEIXLER
MATT GALSOR
ANNE GERMANACOS
SETH GREENLAND
STEVEN LAVINE
ERIC LAX
TOM LUTZ
SUSAN MORSE
CAROL POLAKOFF
JON WIENER
JAIME WOLF

If you would like to help, too, contact Korama Danquah (korama@lareviewofbooks.org)

Panic

PAUL LISICKY

You'd traveled, half naked, in the middle of the night, from the north wing of the hospital to the south. You stumbled past desks, guards, nurses stations, people who were supposed to keep an eye on you, and because you made them look bad they locked you in the special chair.

I didn't know what I'd find when I walked into the room. I said, *they're not trying to hurt you, Dad, please, they care about you,* if only because I needed to think that in order to stand myself.

Listen to me, you said, *listen,* and banged the table with such force I was surprised you didn't break both hands. *Get out of here,* you said calmly, and banged again. *They'll get you too.* Your eyes leveled me with such fury. You wanted to show me you could still hurt someone. And when you said *get out* again, I behaved exactly as you wanted me to, and left you there.

DIANA DEL ÁNGEL (Mexico City, 1982) is a poet, essayist, and human rights defender. She has received creative writing grants from the Fundación para las Letras Mexicanas (Foundation for Mexican Literature) and from the FONCA (Mexico's national fund for culture and the arts). She is the author of the poetry collection *Vasija* (2013) and has published numerous articles on literature in Mexican journals; her second book, *Barranca*, received an honorable mention from the Dolores Castro national poetry prize in 2013. She is currently pursuing a PhD in literature.

ARI BANIAS is the author of *Anybody* (W.W. Norton, September 2016). His poems appear or are forthcoming in *Boston Review, PEN Poetry Series, Poetry, A Public Space*, and elsewhere. He lives in Berkeley, California.

SUZANNE BERNE'S most recent novel is *The Dogs of Littlefield.*

DAVID BIESPIEL'S ninth book, *A Long High Whistle*, received the Frances Fuller Victor Award. Recent books include *Charming Gardeners* and *The Book of Men and Women*. He's a contributor to *The Rumpus, American Poetry Review, Poetry, Partisan, New Republic, Politico, The New York Times*, and *Slate*.

J. MALCOLM GARCIA is a freelance writer and author of *The Khaarijee: A Chronicle of Friendship and War in Kabul* and *What Wars Leave Behind: The Faceless and the Forgotten.* He is a recipient of the Studs Terkel Prize for writing about the working classes and the Sigma Delta Chi Award for excellence in journalism. His work has been anthologized in *Best American Essays, Best American Travel Writing* and *Best American Nonrequired Reading.*

PETER GIZZI is the author of six collections, including *Threshold Songs and In Defense of Nothing: Selected Poems 1987-2011*. A new book, *Archeophonics*, is forthcoming fall of 2016.

RACHEL ELIZA GRIFFITHS is a poet and visual artist. Her most recent collection of poetry, *Lighting the Shadow* (Four Way Books), was published in 2015. Griffiths teaches at Sarah Lawrence College and the Institute of American Indian Arts. She lives in Brooklyn.

LEE GULYAS is a senior lecturer at Western Washington University, where she is also faculty in the Service-Learning Study Abroad Program to Rwanda. She received a 2014 Grants for Artists award, and her work has appeared in journals including *The Common, Prime Number, Kahini Magazine, Tinderbox, Literary Mama, Sweet, Full Grown People*, and *reDIVIDer*.

RICHIE HOFMANN is the author of *Second Empire* (Alice James Books, 2015), winner of the Beatrice Hawley Award. He is the recipient of a Ruth Lilly Poetry Fellowship, and his poems appear in *The New Yorker, Ploughshares, The New Republic,* and *Poetry*. He is co-editor of *Lightbox Poetry*, an online educational resource for students and teachers of contemporary poetry.

VANESSA HUA is author of *Deceit and Other Possibilities* (Willow Books). She is a columnist for the *San Francisco Chronicle* and her two novels are forthcoming from Ballantine. She writes primarily about Asia and the diaspora. She received a Rona Jaffe Foundation Writers' Award, the San Francisco Foundation's James D. Phelan Award for Fiction, and was a Steinbeck Fellow in Creative Writing at San Jose State University. Her fiction and nonfiction has appeared in *The Atlantic, The New York Times, PRI's The World, ZYZZYVA, Guernica*, and elsewhere.

M. J. IUPPA lives on a small farm near the shores of Lake Ontario. She is director of the Visual and Performing Arts Minor at St. John Fisher College. Her lyric essays have appeared in *In Brief: Short Takes on the Personal*, edited by Mary Paumier Jones and Judith Kitchen (Norton, 1999), *Short Takes: Brief Encounters with Contemporary Nonfiction*, edited by Judith Kitchen (Norton, 2005) and *Brief Encounters: A Collection of Contemporary Nonfiction*, edited by Judith Kitchen and Dinah Lenney (Norton, 2015), and her third full-length collection *Small Worlds Floating* is forthcoming from Cherry Grove Collections, August 2016.

Born and raised in Los Angeles, NANCY JOOYOUN KIM is a graduate of UCLA and the MFA Creative Writing Program at the University of Washington, Seattle. Her work has appeared or is forthcoming in *The Margins, Electric Literature's Okey-Panky, The Offing, Apogee Journal's Perigee, The Butter, Prairie Schooner blog*, and elsewhere. She lives in the San Francisco Bay Area where she's working on a novel and personal essays.

MICHAEL KLEIN'S fourth book of poems (and some prose) is *When I Was a Twin* (Sibling Rivalry Press), and his current work appears in *Ploughshares*. He is currently working on a manuscript called *The Early Minutes of Without* and teaches at Goddard College in Vermont and Hunter College in New York City, where he lives.

JOANNA KLINK is the author of four books of poetry, most recently *Excerpts from a Secret Prophecy.*

PAUL LISICKY is the author of five books, including *The*

Narrow Door, a *New York Times* Editor's Choice; *Unbuilt Projects;* and *The Burning House.* A 2016 Guggenheim Fellow, his work has appeared in *The Atlantic, BuzzFeed, Conjunctions*, and other magazines and anthologies. He teaches in the MFA Program at Rutgers University-Camden.

NATHANIEL MACKEY recently published the full-length poetry collection *Blue Fasa* (New Directions, 2015) and the chapbook *Moment's Omen* (Selva Oscura, 2015). *Late Arcade,* volume five of his ongoing prose work *From a Broken Bottle Traces of Perfume Still Emanate*, is forthcoming from New Directions in 2017. He lives in Durham, North Carolina, and teaches at Duke University. He received the Bollingen Prize for American Poetry in 2015.

ANTHONY MCCANN is the author of several collections of poetry, including *Thing Music* and *I Heart Your Fate*. He lives in the Mojave Desert.

REBECCA MCCLANAHAN'S 10 books include *The Tribal Knot, Word Painting*, and *The Riddle Song and Other Rememberings*, winner of the Glasgow Award. Her work has appeared in *Kenyon Review, Boulevard, The Sun, The Best American Essays*, the *Pushcart Prize* anthology, and other publications. She teaches in the MFA programs of Queens University and Rainier Writing Workshop.

BRENDA MILLER is the author of several essay collections, including *An Earlier Life; Listening Against the Stone; Blessing of the Animals;* and *Season of the Body*. She also co-authored *Tell It Slant: Creating, Refining, and Publishing Creative Nonfiction* and *The Pen and The Bell: Mindful Writing in a Busy World.* Her work has received six Pushcart Prizes. She is a professor of English at Western Washington University, and associate faculty at the Rainier Writing Workshop.

ROBIN MYERS (New York, 1987) translates Latin American literature and writes poetry. In 2009 she was named a fellow of the American Literary Translators Association (ALTA); in 2014, she was awarded a residency at the Banff Literary Translation Centre (BILTC) to translate the work of Argentine poet Alejandro Crotto; she was also a resident writer at the Vermont Studio Center in 2015. She is the first-place poetry winner of the 2016 Enizagam Contest and is currently based in Mexico City.

Born in California, DIANA KHOI NGUYEN is currently a PhD candidate in creative writing at the University of Denver. Her poems appear or are forthcoming in *Poetry, American Poetry Review, PEN America, The Iowa Review,* and elsewhere.

AZAREEN VAN DER VLIET OLOOMI is the author of *Fra Keeler.* She is the recipient of a 2015 Whiting Writers' Award and a National Book Foundation "5 Under 35" honoree.

TOM STEVENSON is Middle East and North Africa correspondent for *Deutsche Welle* and *The Globe and Mail* based in Istanbul and Cairo.

ABIGAIL THOMAS'S latest book is a memoir, *What Comes Next and How To Like It.*

ANNA ROSE WELCH is an editor and violinist in Erie, Pennsylvania. She holds an MFA from Bowling Green State University. Her work has appeared in *Best New Poets 2014, The Kenyon Review Online, Guernica, Crab Orchard Review, Barrow Street, Tupelo Quarterly,* and elsewhere. She was the winner of the 2016 Alice James Award. Her first book, *We, the Almighty Fires,* will be published by Alice James Books in 2018.

Included throughout are images from the new four-volume book series *Emerging from the Shadows: A Survey of Women Artists Working in California, 1860–1960* (Schiffer Publishing), by Maurine St. Gaudens, which explores the careers of 320 women artists, many previously unrecorded in the annals of art history. Biographical information on the life of each artist is presented with images of her works culled from private and public collections.

Syracuse University Press

SyracuseUniversityPress.syr.edu

800-848-6224

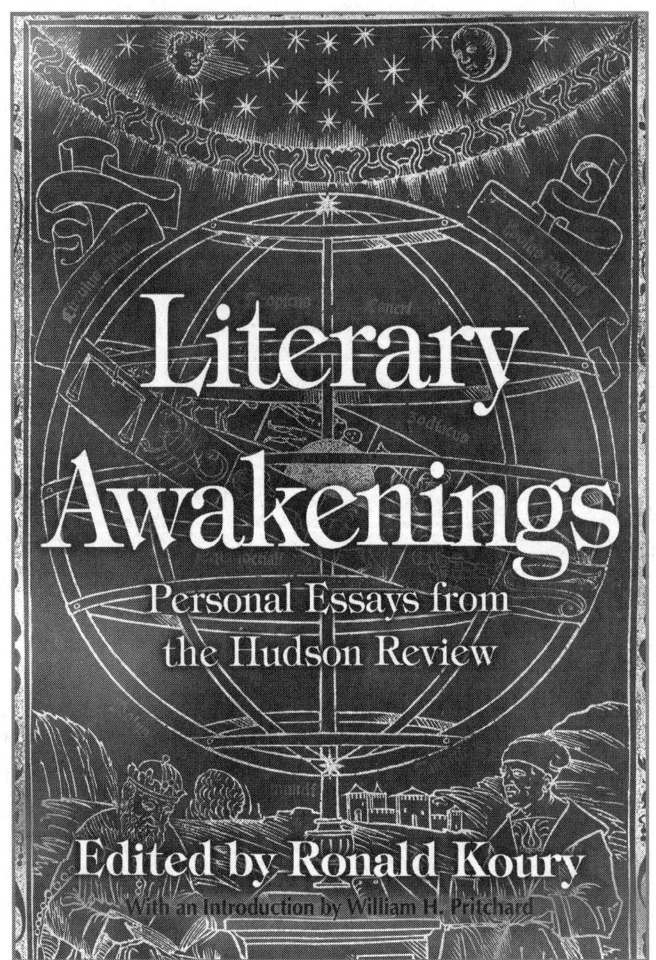

"The collection makes a strong case for the centrality of reading to human life . . . to argue for literature's importance in an increasingly post-literate age."

—Jeff Porter, University of Iowa

The essays gathered here recall disparate awakenings to the influence of literature and discoveries of the many ways in which it enriches nearly every aspect of our lives.

Paper $24.95 978-0-8156-1078-6

ebook 978-0-8156-5385-1